YORK NOTES

General Editors: Professor A.N. Jeffares (*University of Stirling*) & Professor Suheil Bushrui (*American University of Beirut*)

William Shakespeare

ROMEO AND JULIET

Notes by N.H. Keeble

BA (LAMPETER) D PHIL (OXFORD)
Lecturer in English, University of Stirling

LONGMAN
YORK PRESS

The illustrations of the Globe Playhouse are from *The Globe Restored in Theatre: A Way of Seeing* by C. Walter Hodges, published by Oxford University Press
© Oxford University Press

YORK PRESS
Immeuble Esseily, Place Riad Solh, Beirut.

LONGMAN GROUP UK LIMITED
Longman House, Burnt Mill, Harlow,
Essex CM20 2JE, England
Associated companies, branches and representatives
throughout the world

© Librairie du Liban 1980

First published 1980
Eighteenth impression 1994

ISBN 0-582-02302-5

Produced by Longman Singapore Publishers Pte Ltd
Printed in Singapore

Contents

Part 1

Introduction

Shakespeare's life and times

We know that Shakespeare was baptised in Holy Trinity Church at Stratford-upon-Avon on 26 April 1564 and that he was buried there on 25 April 1616, but we know for certain very little more about the life of the greatest English dramatist and poet. Shakespeare's name does appear on some forty official documents and his family is mentioned in many others; he is named occasionally by some of his contemporary dramatists and writers; and, later in the seventeenth century, a good deal of gossip about him was recorded. From these sources we can make out the main lines of his life, but only so far as his public activities are concerned. His inner life, how he thought about his plays, his beliefs, prejudices and the like, these are hidden from us. Not until another 50 years had passed did writers begin to record their own lives, and it was not until the eighteenth century that auto-biography became at all common. Hence, it is not surprising that Shakespeare himself tells us nothing of his imaginative and artistic life. As a result, many scholars have tried to detect in the plays clues to Shakespeare's character and thoughts, but this is a very difficult thing to do. Shakespeare submerges himself in the characters he creates to a greater extent than any other writer. His ability to imagine and recreate so many different people with their different emotions and attitudes means that we can never be sure when we read in the plays Shakespeare's own convictions and when we read simply those senti-ments befitting the character who speaks. Shakespeare the man eludes us.

We do know that Shakespeare was born into a well-to-do family in the country market town of Stratford-upon-Avon in Warwickshire. His father, John Shakespeare, was a prosperous trader and merchant and a person of some importance in the town. In 1568 he became high bailiff (or mayor) of Stratford. In 1557 he had married Mary Arden. Their third child and eldest son, William, went to the local grammar school, where he would have studied Latin, history, logic and rhetoric. In November 1582 William, then aged eighteen, married Anne Hathaway, who was twenty-six years old. They had a daughter (Susanna) in May 1583, and twins (Hamnet and Judith) in 1585.

We know little more about Shakespeare than this until he is mentioned in a pamphlet by the playwright Robert Greene in 1592. From this reference we learn that Shakespeare was then an actor and dramatist in London, but when he left Stratford, and why he left, we simply do not know. What he did during these 'lost years', 1585–92, has been much discussed, but nothing has been proved. Robert Greene is cross in his pamphlet because the 'upstart' Shakespeare, of whom he thinks little, is setting himself up as the equal of established London dramatists. To have aroused this hostility from a competitor, Shakespeare must, by 1592, have been long enough in London to have made a name for himself as a dramatist. We may guess, therefore, that he left Stratford in 1586 or 1587, but it is only a guess.

During the next 20 years Shakespeare continued to live in London, visiting his wife and family in Stratford each year. He continued to act, but his chief fame was as a playwright. His plays were very popular and brought him considerable wealth. He was able to buy lands around Stratford, and a large house in the town, to which he retired in 1611. He died there on 23 April 1616.

The Elizabethan Renaissance

For whatever reason Shakespeare went to London, he could hardly have chosen a better time if he wanted to be a dramatist. This was the beginning of the 'golden age' of English literature, the Elizabethan Renaissance. Although Elizabeth reigned as queen from 1558 to 1603, the term 'Elizabethan' is used very loosely in a literary sense to refer to the period 1580 to 1625, when the great works of the age were produced. (Some critics distinguish the later part of this period as 'Jacobean' from the name of the king who succeeded Elizabeth, James I, who reigned from 1603 to 1625). The poet Edmund Spenser had heralded the new age with his pastoral poem *The Shepheards Calender* (1579), and his friend Sir Philip Sidney had explained the new theories of poetry in his essay *The Apologie for Poetrie* (written about 1580, although not published until 1595). Spenser's great allegorical epic poem *The Faerie Queene* began to appear from 1590, the year in which Sidney's immensely influential prose romance *Arcadia* was published. These two writers established a new set of literary ideals, and a host of other poets strove to imitate them and go beyond what they had accomplished.

But this was not only the great age of poetry. The poetic achievements of the Elizabethans may have been equalled by later poets, but their drama has had no rivals. There had been no theatres during the medieval period and plays were then strictly of a religious nature, performed at Christian festivals by amateur actors. Such professional actors as there were wandered the country, putting on a variety of entertainments in the yards of inns, on make-shift stages in market squares, or anywhere else suitable. They did not perform full length plays, but mimes, juggling and comedy acts. Such actors were generally regarded as little better than vagabonds and layabouts.

Just before Shakespeare went to London all this began to change. A number of young men who had been to the universities of Oxford and Cambridge came to London in the 1580s and began to write plays which made use of what they had learned about the classical drama of ancient Greece and Rome. Plays such as John Lyly's *Alexander and Campaspe* (1584), Christopher Marlowe's *Tamburlaine the Great* (about 1587) and Thomas Kyd's *The Spanish Tragedy* (1588–9) were unlike anything that had been written in English before. These dramatists and their fellow 'university wits', as they are called, brought a new life, vigour and sophistication to English drama. With the exception of Lyly, who wrote in prose, they wrote in blank verse, not rhymed verse like the old religious drama, and so had greater freedom of expression. They adopted many of the conventions of the classical drama (like the Chorus, which we find in *Romeo and Juliet*). And they wrote on subjects that were not religious, so opening up all history and legend as suitable matter for plays.

These were the men, who had revitalised English drama, whom Shakespeare challenged when he came to London. Robert Greene was one of them, and we have heard how little he liked this Shakespeare (who had not even been to a university!) setting himself up as a dramatist. The most important change of all, however, was that they wrote for the professional theatres. In 1576 James Burbage built the first permanent theatre in England just outside London. It was called simply 'The Theatre'. Others soon followed. Thus, when Shakespeare came to London, there was a flourishing drama, theatres and companies of actors waiting for him, such as there had never been before in England.

The Elizabethan theatre

The Elizabethan stage

These Elizabethan theatres were not like the ones we know today. Their form derived from the inn yards and animal baiting rings in which actors had been accustomed to perform in the past. They were circular wooden buildings with a paved courtyard in the middle open to the sky. A rectangular stage jutted out from the side of the building into the middle of this yard. Some of the audience stood in the yard (or 'pit') to watch the play. They were thus on three sides of the stage, and much closer to it than an audience sitting in a modern theatre. These 'groundlings' paid only a penny to get in, but for wealthier spectators there were seats in three covered tiers or balconies in the sides of the building overlooking the pit and the stage. Shakespeare aptly called such a theatre a 'wooden O' in the Prologue to *Henry V* (line 13).

The stage itself was partially covered by a roof which projected from the wall at the rear of the stage and was supported by two posts in front. On either side at the back of the stage was a door. These led to the dressing room (or 'tiring house') and it was by means of these doors that actors entered and left the stage. Between the doors was a small recess or alcove which was curtained off. This might, indeed, be simply another, middle, doorway into the tiring house. Such a 'discovery place', as it was called, would serve, for example, for Juliet's room in IV.3–5 of *Romeo and Juliet*. Juliet would deliver her soliloquy in IV.3 on the stage and at the end of it, as the stage direction tells us, she would lie on her bed in the discovery place. The curtains would then be pulled across. Act IV Scene 4 would be played on the main stage, and, at the end of the scene, the Nurse would go to the back of the stage and pull the curtains to find (or 'discover' in Elizabethan English) Juliet apparently 'dead' in bed. Such discovery places were too small to allow any acting in them. In *Romeo and Juliet* Juliet merely lies on the bed, while the characters in IV.5 lament their grief on the main stage. When these characters go out, there is a stage direction telling the Nurse to close the curtains again (IV.5.95). Juliet would then go into the tiring house while the rest of the scene continued on the main stage. The discovery place might also have served for the Capulet vault in V.3. Above the discovery place was a balcony. This might be used as a privileged place for noblemen or high-paying spectators to sit (such people might, indeed, actually sit on seats around the edge of the stage), but it was also used, for example, for scenes like the balcony scenes in *Romeo and Juliet* (II.2 and III.5).

Such 'public theatres', as they are called, could hold about 3,000 spectators. The yards were about 70ft in diameter and the rectangular stages approximately 40ft by 30ft and 5ft 6in high. There were, however, also smaller rectangular, indoor theatres, more like present-day theatres. In these, which held about 700 people, there were seats for all the members of the audience, facilities for elaborate stage effects and, because they were enclosed, artificial lighting could be used. The plays written for these 'private theatres' differed from those written for the public theatres. As it cost more to go to a private theatre, the audience came from a higher social class than that at the public theatres, and such a select audience demanded a sophisticated and elaborate kind of play. Shakespeare's last plays were written for such a theatre (the Blackfriars Theatre, bought by Shakespeare's company in 1608), but *Romeo and Juliet* was written for the public theatre. Shakespeare's company performed at James Burbage's Theatre until 1596, and used the Swan and the Curtain until they moved into their own new theatre, the Globe, in 1599. We know *Romeo and Juliet* was played at the Curtain, and, as a popular play, it would have been presented at the Globe as well.

THE GLOBE PLAYHOUSE

The theatre, originally built by James Burbage in 1576, was made of wood (Burbage had been trained as a carpenter). It was situated to the north of the River Thames on Shoreditch in Finsbury Fields. There was trouble with the lease of the land, and so the theatre was dismantled in 1598, and reconstructed 'in an other forme' on the south side of the Thames as the Globe. Its sign is thought to have been a figure of the Greek hero Hercules carrying the globe. It was built in six months, its galleries being roofed with thatch. This caught fire in 1613 when some smouldering wadding, from a cannon used in a performance of Shakespeare's *Henry VIII*, lodged in it. The theatre was burnt down, and when it was rebuilt again on the old foundations, the galleries were roofed with tiles.

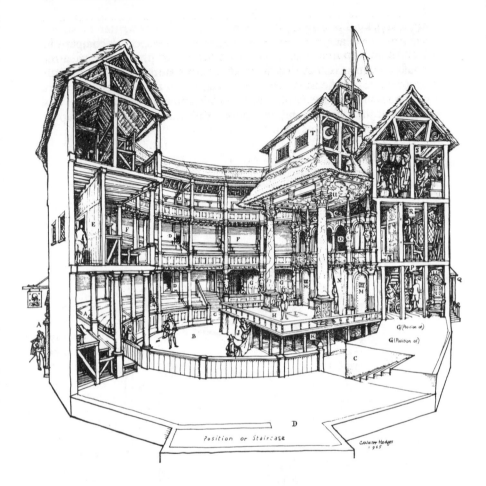

A CONJECTURAL RECONSTRUCTION OF THE INTERIOR OF THE GLOBE PLAYHOUSE

AA Main entrance
B The Yard
CC Entrances to lowest gallery
D Entrance to staircase and upper galleries
E Corridor serving the different sections of the middle gallery
F Middle gallery ('Twopenny Rooms')
G 'Gentlemen's Rooms or Lords Rooms'
H The stage
J The hanging being put up round the stage
K The 'Hell' under the stage
L The stage trap, leading down to the Hell
MM Stage doors

N Curtained 'place behind the stage'
O Gallery above the stage, used as required sometimes by musicians, sometimes by spectators, and often as part of the play
P Back-stage area (the tiring-house)
Q Tiring-house door
R Dressing-rooms
S Wardrobe and storage
T The hut housing the machine for lowering enthroned gods, etc., to the stage
U The 'Heavens'
W Hoisting the playhouse flag

Elizabethan performances

The most important thing to remember about performances in the public theatres is that they were continuous and there was very little scenery. Scene divisions were only added to most of Shakespeare's plays much later by eighteenth-century editors. The Elizabethan editions of *Romeo and Juliet* have neither act nor scene divisions. These divisions are still retained in modern editions of the plays because they make reference easier, but they should not mislead the student into supposing there was any real break in the play such as there is in the theatre today when the curtains are closed and the set is changed. A modern audience might well grow impatient with waiting for the frequent scene changes during Act IV of *Romeo and Juliet*. Such a succession of short scenes would not have delayed an Elizabethan performance at all, when the scenes would have carried straight on. 'Continuous staging' means that an Elizabethan performance would have been shorter than a modern one: in the Prologue to *Romeo and Juliet* the Chorus speaks of 'two hours' as the acting time (line 12; compare *Henry VIII*, Prologue, line 13).

We can see the kind of thing that happened from the stage directions in *Romeo and Juliet*. In I.4 Romeo and his friends decide to go to Capulet's party. At the end of the scene they 'march about the stage' while the serving-men come on to begin I.5. This represents their going in to Capulet's house: there would have been no break in the actual performance. Again, in II.1 Mercutio and Benvolio are looking for Romeo. Failing to find him, they leave, and he 'comes forward' to begin II.2. His first line actually makes a rhyming verse couplet with Benvolio's last line of II.1. Clearly, although the scene of the action has changed (Mercutio and Benvolio are outside Capulet's garden; Romeo is inside it), there is no break in the play. Romeo comes straight on. A different kind of example occurs in III.5. This begins 'aloft', as the stage direction puts it, that is, on the balcony at the rear of the stage. When Romeo has left by climbing down to the stage, which here represents the garden (III.5.42), Juliet comes down by the stairs to the tiring house and enters the stage through one of the rear doors to meet her mother in the house (III.5.64–5). In this scene, then, the stage has represented two different places (the garden and the interior of the house) but the acting goes on regardless.

It is because of this continuous staging and the lack of scenery that characters in Shakespeare's plays often tell the audience what locality the stage represents at different moments. Romeo's last words in II.2, for example, set the scene for II.3. Similarly, Romeo's words at II.2.107–8 create the scene in the imagination of the audience. On the other hand, we often cannot tell where a scene is set. There is no evidence in the text, for example, for the locality of I.2 or II.4 of *Romeo and Juliet*. Modern editors often supply a locale for such scenes, but we can be confident that if Shakespeare's characters do not tell us where they are it does not matter much. The lack of a curtain across the stage in the Elizabethan theatre explains why scenes often end with rhyming lines. These show the audience that the scene *has* ended, and prepare them for a new scene (for example, the final two lines of V.1 in *Romeo and Juliet*). And because actors were in full view from the moment they set foot on the stage, entrances and exits had to be written in as part of the play. Actors could not come on to the stage and get ready for a scene; it would seem very odd for them only to begin speaking once everyone was in position. That is why characters always say that they are coming or going, to cover these movements (for example, in our play, I.3.1–5; I.4.113–4; I.5.144). For the same reason, dead bodies had always to be removed by the actors in the course of the play (so Mercutio goes off-stage to die and Tybalt's body is carried off, III.1.108, 196).

We can see, then, that the nature of the theatre for which Shakespeare wrote affected his plays in a number of ways. It is as an attempt to return to the simplicity and swiftness of an Elizabethan production that modern productions of Shakespeare tend to do without the elaborate scenery that was characteristic of the presentations of his plays in the last century. And it is to recapture the intimacy of the involvement of the audience with the actors that a number of modern theatres have done away with the proscenium arch which rigidly separates the audience from the stage. A stage which projects into the auditorium is now often preferred. We should remember this modern tendency to return to the Elizabethan model if ever we are tempted to think that Shakespeare's theatre was primitive.

Shakespeare's dramatic career

The dates of the plays

For such theatres Shakespeare wrote between about 1588 and 1613 thirty-seven plays, as well as contributing to some by other dramatists. This was by no means an exceptional number for a professional playwright of the times. Shakespeare's friend and fellow dramatist Ben Jonson wrote nearly twenty plays and many more masques, Philip Massinger wrote nearly forty plays, and their contemporary Thomas Heywood claimed to have had a hand in 220 plays! The order in which these plays were written, and their dates, are matters of doubt. Some of his plays were published before Shakespeare's death, but in these cases, although of course the plays must have been written before they were published, we do not know how long before. Sometimes there are references to contemporary events in the plays themselves which help us to date them. The difficulty, though, is recognising such references. When, in *Romeo and Juliet* I.3.24–36, the Nurse speaks of an earthquake eleven years ago, is Shakespeare reminding his audience of the earthquake that actually occurred in London in 1580? If we knew that he was, we could date the play to 1591, but we cannot be sure. We can be more confident when we know when a play was first performed. It must have been written shortly before this. Unfortunately, the first performances of many of Shakespeare's plays are not recorded. Often, scholars can only argue for a date on the basis of their understanding of the development of Shakespeare's art. They will say that a certain passage of poetry sounds 'early' rather than 'late'. This method of dating is, however, complicated by the fact that Shakespeare seems to have revised a number of his plays some years after they were first written. We can thus find in one play seemingly 'early' and 'late' verse.

Shakespeare's development

Despite these difficulties over the dating of individual plays, the broad lines of Shakespeare's dramatic career are now plain. He began in the late 1580s and early 1590s by rewriting old plays. As he moved on to write his own plays, he concentrated on comedies which depended for their effect upon funny situations and surprises (like *The Comedy of Errors*, 1590–3) and plays dealing with English history (like the three plays of *Henry VI*, 1589–91). This was the period of his apprenticeship. During the 1590s he developed his mastery of these kinds of play to write comic masterpieces such as *As You Like It* (1599–1600) and *Twelfth Night* (1599–1600) and history plays such as *Henry IV* (1596–8) and *Henry V* (1598–9).

As the century ends, however, a new and more sombre note enters his work. Plays such as *Troilus and Cressida* (1601–2) and *Measure for Measure* (1603–4) do not seem to know whether they are comedies or tragedies. *Measure for Measure* ends happily, but it is not very funny; *Troilus and Cressida* does not end happily, but it is often very funny. As we cannot be sure how to react, the plays of this period are often called 'problem plays'. But then in the early 1600s we have the period of Shakespeare's great tragedies – *Hamlet* (1600–1), *Othello* (1602–3), *King Lear* (1605–6) and *Macbeth* (1605–6). Because of the different mood of these plays this first decade of the seventeenth century is sometimes called Shakespeare's 'Jacobean' phase.

And then, finally, in the last years of his dramatic career, Shakespeare wrote a small group of plays of an entirely new kind. These 'romances', as they are often called, are in many ways the most remarkable of all his plays. The group comprises *Pericles* (1608–9), *Cymbeline* (1609–10), *The Winter's Tale* (1610–11) and *The Tempest* (1611–12). These all have happy endings, but they are not at all like the comedies of the first period. In all of these plays the characters have known or experience great sadness. Shakespeare does not, as in the early comedies, ignore sorrow and suffering, but neither does it threaten to overwhelm him as in the great tragedies. These very beautiful plays all end on a note of hope for the future. Their great theme is reconciliation – a theme we can see already interests Shakespeare in *Romeo and Juliet* (see p.86).

The place of *Romeo and Juliet* in Shakespeare's career

Romeo and Juliet was first published in 1597, so it must have been written before this. The great differences in the style of the play, between, for example, Mercutio's wordplay and Juliet's soliloquy in IV.3, have led some scholars to think that Shakespeare wrote a version of the play very early in his career and then revised it later. Although the stylistic variety is certainly there, most critics now agree that the play was written in 1595, that is, during the first period of Shakespeare's career.

Coming at that early date, the play is a remarkable achievement: it may, indeed, be claimed as Shakespeare's first masterpiece. While it does still have the sheer delight in playing with words which marks Shakespeare's early work (see p.92), and contains scenes in which we may well feel Shakespeare is allowing this delight to run away with him, it has, too, passages of astonishing poetic power and a skill in characterisation which heralds the greatness of Shakespeare's later work.

It is remarkable in another way, too, for it is unusual amongst the early plays in being a tragedy. In *Titus Andronicus* (1592–3) Shakespeare had written a bloodthirsty tragedy of horror in the style then fashionable, and in his history play *Richard III* (1592–3) he had dealt with the rule and death of a villainous king, but neither of these is at all like the poignant and sad tragedy of *Romeo and Juliet. Richard II* (1595–6) is more movingly tragic and does have some of the pathos and inevitability of *Romeo and Juliet,* but, as this is a history play, Richard's reign and death are presented not so much as a personal tragedy as the root cause of civil wars which lasted throughout the fifteenth century. All Shakespeare's other early plays are histories or comedies. Indeed, *Romeo and Juliet* stands out in this respect not only from the early plays, but from all Shakespeare's work. Only once again, in the last of the great tragedies, *Antony and Cleopatra* (1606–7), was he to write a tragedy based upon the passion of two lovers for each other, a passion which blinds them to the world and their normal responsibilities and duties.

As the play is so unusual we may ask why it was Shakespeare chose then to turn aside from comedies and histories to write it. We cannot know the answer to this question, but there is some evidence that the main concerns of *Romeo and Juliet* were then in his mind. At just this time, in *A Midsummer Night's Dream* (1595–6), he wrote a comedy on the blindness and irresistible power of sudden love. In this play we are entertained by the confusions caused by the fairy Puck amongst several pairs of lovers. By anointing their eyes with the magic juice of a flower Puck makes them fall in love with the first person they see, and so everyone's affections get muddled up. This may not sound much like *Romeo and Juliet*, and it is certainly a very different kind of play. But although in *A Midsummer Night's Dream* Shakespeare makes fun of the passions and changes of heart which love brings, this is neverthe-less the very theme of the very different, and tragic, play of *Romeo and Juliet* written at the same time. We remember that at the beginning of the play Romeo is infatuated with Rosaline. Suddenly, he transfers his affection completely and unalterably to Juliet, and the two lovers are from then on blind to all else. Just so Puck's lovers suddenly change their allegiance, and are blind to all save the person they first see. Other than noting this similarity between the two plays we can go no further in answering our question of why Shakespeare should have written this tragedy at this stage in his career. The workings of Shakespeare's mind are indeed hidden from us.

The publication of the plays

Quartos

Nineteen of Shakespeare's plays were printed during his lifetime in what are called 'quartos' from the fact that these books, which each contained one play, were made up of sheets of paper each folded twice to make four leaves. Shakespeare, however, did not supervise the publication of these plays. This was not unusual. When a playwright sold a play to a dramatic company he sold all his rights in it. There was then no copyright protection for an author, so a writer had no control over what happened to his work. Anyone who could get hold of the text of a play from a playhouse might print it if he wanted to. Actors (or even members of the audience) might publish what they could remember of the text of a play. Clearly, texts produced like this would be very unreliable.

Furthermore, the quality of the printing was very poor. No one then thought of stage-plays as 'great literature', and so printers only produced them as cheaply and quickly as they could for a quick popular sale (the quartos cost only sixpence). As a result, they were very careless about correcting printing errors. Not until Ben Jonson collected all his plays together and carefully supervised their publication in a large edition of his *Works* in 1616 had anyone thought mere plays deserved such attention.

The First Folio

In 1623 John Heming and Henry Condell, two actors in Shakespeare's company, collected together thirty-six of Shakespeare's plays (*Pericles* was omitted) and published them, like Jonson's plays, in a large folio (so called since in such a book the sheets of paper are folded once to give two leaves). This, the First Folio, was followed by later editions in 1632, 1663 and 1685. These folios are now among the most valued possessions of our libraries, but their texts still present many difficulties. Shakespeare, of course, was not still alive to check the text of the First Folio. Furthermore, the plays as printed in the Folio often differ from the earlier quartos, leaving a modern editor with the problem of deciding which version is nearest to Shakespeare's original playscript. In addition, there are still many printing errors. It is because editors correct these errors in different ways, and sometimes prefer the quarto text, sometimes the Folio text, that different modern editions of Shakespeare's plays vary.

The text of *Romeo and Juliet*

Romeo and Juliet was published in a quarto in 1597 and again in 1599 (these two editions are distinguished as Q1 and Q2). Q1 is a 'bad quarto': it prints the text of the play as two or three of the actors who took part in a performance remembered it. Such a memorised version is obviously unreliable. But although Q1 is short and often confused, it does reflect an actual performance of Shakespeare's time. It has unusually full stage directions and must often record what the actors actually said and did on the stage. (Q1 is printed as an appendix in *Romeo and Juliet*, edited by H.H. Furness, New Variorum Edition of Shakespeare, New York, 1963.)

Q2, on the other hand, is based upon a written copy of the play, but although it is fuller and more reliable than Q1, it still has many errors. For example, the four lines II.2.188–91 are printed not only there but again in Q2 at the beginning of the Friar's speech which opens II.3. A modern editor has to decide in which place he thinks Shakespeare meant them to be. Nor does Q2 always make clear who is speaking: the parts of the musicians at the end of IV.5, for example, are not clearly distinguished.

It may even have been Shakespeare's own manuscript that the printer of Q2 worked with, for quite often it prints what appears to be a rough draft of lines, followed by a second version. For example, I.2.14 and 15 look like two versions of the same line. Or again, in Romeo's long speech to the Friar in III.3, lines 40–4 repeat themselves, using almost the same words. Almost certainly, Shakespeare did not intend this repetition and meant one or other of the lines to be left out. It looks as though the printer did not notice that one of the lines had been crossed out. One passage of a play in Shakespeare's handwriting is extant. It is his contribution of nearly 150 lines to *Sir Thomas More*, a play by other dramatists. This is reprinted as an appendix in Shakespeare's *Complete Works*, edited by Peter Alexander (London, 1951), and a glance at it will show the kind of difficulties the printer of Q2 probably dealt with: spelling, corrections, line and speech divisions all present problems in this manuscript as Shakespeare left it.

A third edition (Q3, 1609) was based on Q2, and so were a fourth (Q4, 1622) and a fifth (Q5, 1637). These texts contain some corrections of errors in Q2, but we cannot know if they were simply the printer's guesses or were actually what Shakespeare wrote. Besides, they carried on many of the old errors, and added new ones of their own. The Folio text of 1623 was based on Q3. A modern editor therefore works with Q1 and Q2 as the earliest versions on which all the others are based. He will make Q2 his main text (as the fuller version), and will check it against Q1 when he suspects an error. He will also see if later versions offer a possible correction in such cases.

As an example of the difficulties, we may notice the variation in only one word in the printed texts. Romeo addresses Juliet in II.2.167. What he says appears like this in the different editions:

Q1   Madame?
Q2, Q3, F1 My Neece?
Q4, Q5   My Deere?
F2, F3, F4 My Sweet?

In the modernised Penguin edition, 'neece' is preferred and spelled 'nyas', but other modern editors print 'sweet'. When only one word appears so variously we can see that the editor has many decisions to make in preparing a complete text.

Shakespeare's use of sources

We are accustomed to the idea that a writer should invent all his own work. We value originality. Once a book has been published, its text belongs to the author, and no one may copy it or borrow from it without his consent. It comes as something of a surprise, therefore, to find that in Shakespeare's time, and for hundreds of years earlier, it was not thought at all wrong to copy a story from another author. Medieval writers, indeed, were frequently anxious to point out that they had *not* invented their stories, but took them from an earlier author. Clearly, they had a very different idea of 'originality' from our own! What they valued was not the invention of a new story but the way the author told an old story. Hence, throughout the medieval and Renaissance periods, stories were repeated, enlarged and embellished as they were treated again and again by writers from many countries. Looking back from the present, we can see all the writers of Europe collaborating together over many centuries.

Romeo and Juliet is an excellent example of this process. Shakespeare, like his contemporary dramatists, seldom invented the plots of his plays. He usually borrowed them from older poems, plays or stories, and *Romeo and Juliet* is no exception. But it had already been borrowed several times before it came to Shakespeare's turn. The story of the two lovers was first written in Italian by Masuccio Salernitano in 1476, and was rewritten several times by Italian and French authors during the next hundred years. In 1562 the English poet Arthur Brooke, who had read it in French and Italian, published a long poem called *The Tragicall Historye of Romeus and Juliet.* This was the main source for Shakespeare's play, but Shakespeare also knew, and used, a later English prose version of the story by William Painter. Painter included 'The goodly History of the true and constant love between Rhomeo and Julietta' in a collection of tales he published in 1567 called *Palace of Pleasure.* There was also an English play on this subject, which Brooke mentions in the preface to his poem. Shakespeare may very well have seen it, may even, indeed, have had a copy of it by him as he worked on his own play. If so, we cannot tell what he owed to it, as the old play no longer exists. But we can see that he owes a very great deal to Brooke's poem.

However, it is the differences between Shakespeare's play and Brooke's poem, rather than the similarities, which are interesting, for the changes Shakespeare made to the story as told by Brooke must have been deliberate. They therefore show us something of how Shakespeare worked, what he was trying to do.

We may, for the sake of convenience, list the principal changes as follows:

(*i*) In Brooke's poem the story lasts nine months; in Shakespeare's play it is compressed into a few days. This stresses the remarkable suddenness of the lovers' passion. It has no time to develop: it completely overwhelms Romeo and Juliet the moment they see each other. The compression of time also makes the love of Romeo and Juliet seem even more fragile, and so increases the tragedy. Their affection has no sooner come than it is destroyed. After their first meeting and marriage the next day, they do not have a moment of undisturbed happiness. Troubles beset them from the start and, instead of being spread over several months, they come one upon the heels of the next with no relief and no escape. Because events happen so quickly, we have a sense that the lovers are trapped, that their final deaths are inevitable. (This is discussed further on pp.73–5, and, to make the time-scale clear, the timing of each scene is given at the beginning of each scene summary.)

(*ii*) Only in Shakespeare's play does Paris come to Juliet's tomb. This shows us that Paris does have a true affection for Juliet, and, if we read the final scene of the play, we can see how effective it is to have Juliet's two suitors meet at the climax of the play. Paris has been in the background throughout the play and has, unknowingly, contributed much to the unhappiness of Juliet. Here, he too is suddenly caught up by events and destroyed by them. That he too, the Prince's kinsman, should die, increases the regret of the Capulets and Montagues and the Prince himself, and strengthens our sense of the waste of the tragedy.

(*iii*) The character of Mercutio is entirely Shakespeare's invention. In the earlier versions of the story, Mercutio plays a very small part. His importance as a contrast to Romeo will be discussed later (pp.103–4).

(*iv*) Similarly, Shakespeare develops the characters of the Nurse and Tybalt. By doing this, he makes his play more convincing (since fully developed characters are more interesting than flat ones); he introduces a variety of mood with the comedy of the Nurse and the anger of Tybalt; and he is able both to highlight Juliet's character by contrasting her with the Nurse and also to set Tybalt as a foil against Romeo and Benvolio (see pp.105–6).

(*v*) Shakespeare makes Juliet younger. In Brooke's poem she is sixteen, but in the play she is not yet fourteen. This increases Juliet's vulnerability: we feel the more pity for her because she is so young and inexperienced. More than this, though, we notice her development from a young and submissive girl who is very ready to obey her parents early in the play, to a self-reliant, defiant and tragic heroine who knows her own mind at the end. By stressing her youth Shakespeare stresses this contrast between Juliet's character before and after she has met Romeo. He makes her early obedience to her parents the more credible and her later resolution to defy them the more remarkable. (Juliet's development is discussed on p.102.)

We should also remember, of course, that Shakespeare added to the story his poetry. In every scene this affects us in many different ways, so that to read *Romeo and Juliet* is an entirely different – and much richer – experience than reading Brooke's poem.

A note on the text

All references to *Romeo and Juliet* are to T.J.B. Spencer's New Penguin Shakespeare edition of the play, Penguin Books, Harmondsworth, 1967. Act and scene divisions are the same in all modern editions of the play, but line numbers may vary from edition to edition, especially in scenes written in prose. The variation should not, however, be so great as to prevent anyone using a different edition from finding a reference in his text.

All references to Shakespeare's other plays are to the texts printed in William Shakespeare, *The Complete Works,* edited by Peter Alexander, Collins, London and Glasgow, 1951, but again, it should be easy to locate these references in any good edition of Shakespeare.

Part 2

Summaries

of ROMEO AND JULIET

A general summary

In Act I Romeo, infatuated by Rosaline (whom we never meet), goes to the party given by Lord Capulet on Sunday evening in order to see his loved one. There he meets Juliet and, forgetting Rosaline, falls in love with her (I.5). However, the Act ends with the lovers discovering each other's identity, and hence the threatening fact that, as Juliet is a Capulet and Romeo a Montague, they belong to feuding families who would never let them see each other. In Act II the course of their love nevertheless moves quickly. That night, in the famous balcony scene (II.2), they exchange vows, and the following afternoon they are married secretly by Friar Laurence (II.6).

In Act III the tragic counter-movement begins. Romeo had not been invited to Lord Capulet's party, and the Capulet Tybalt is determined not to let this intrusion pass unpunished. In the quarrel and fight that follows in the first scene of Act III Romeo's friend Mercutio is killed by Tybalt and Romeo avenges his friend's death by killing Tybalt. For this, Romeo is banished from Verona by the Prince, Escalus. The Friar advises Romeo to leave Verona to live in the nearby city of Mantua until there is an opportunity to proclaim his marriage to Juliet publicly (III.2), and so, after spending Monday night with Juliet, Romeo leaves (III.5). Juliet's parents mistake her sorrow at Romeo's leaving for grief for her dead cousin, Tybalt, and think to overcome it by insisting that on the next Thursday she should marry her suitor, Count Paris (III.4). This Juliet refuses to do, and her father threatens never to see her again if she persists in this disobedience (III.5).

At the beginning of Act IV Juliet seeks the advice of Friar Laurence. He suggests that the night before her marriage she should take a potion which will make her appear dead on her wedding morning. She would then be placed in the family vault, from which he and Romeo could rescue her when she awakens, and Romeo could take her back to live with him in Mantua. To this she agrees, and so submits to her father who, overjoyed at this change of heart, brings the wedding forward to the next day, Wednesday (IV.2). The Friar meanwhile writes to Romeo to tell him of the scheme and bids him return from Mantua. However, while all else goes according to plan, this letter is never delivered (V.2). Instead, Romeo is told by his servant that Juliet is really dead (V.1). On hearing the news, Romeo returns to the Capulet vault, where Juliet lies, there to poison himself. When Juliet wakes up in the vault, and sees Romeo's body, she stabs herself in her grief. The deaths of both their heirs, explained by Friar Laurence in a summary of the plot (V.3.229–69), reconcile the Capulet and Montague families.

Detailed summaries

Prologue

The Chorus (who also appears in II.1) introduces the matter of the play in a sonnet addressed to the audience. The first four lines (or quatrain) prepare the audience to see the long-standing hostility between two equally noble Veronese families (the Capulets and Montagues) breaking out anew; the second quatrain foretells the healing of this feud through the deaths of a pair of ill-fated lovers, children of these families (Romeo and Juliet). This is to be the matter of the play, which will last two hours. The Chorus concludes in the last two lines (or couplet) by asking the audience to watch with patience while the actors do their best to please them. The stress of the Chorus's introduction is upon the tragic nature of the play – we are not prepared by him for the comic figure of the Nurse or the wit of Mercutio.

NOTES AND GLOSSARY:

Chorus: although the word is taken from classical drama, where the Chorus consists of a group of characters commenting upon the action, the Chorus here is a single figure; Shakespeare used such a Chorus in other plays to prepare the audience to watch favourably, for example *Henry V, Henry VIII* and *Troilus and Cressida*

dignity: noble rank

mutiny: violent quarrelling

where: in which

civil: belonging to citizens and civilised

star-crossed: thwarted by the influence of the stars, ill-fated

misadventured . . . overthrows: unfortunate pitiful disappointments

traffic: business

miss: be wanting, seem to be inadequate in our performance

Act I Scene 1

Time: 9 a.m. Sunday morning (I.1.160–1). [How the day is discovered is explained on p.73.]

The play begins like a comedy, with the witty, boastful and bawdy exchanges of the Capulet servants Sampson and Gregory who, meeting Abram and another Montague servant, embark on a quarrel with them which their evident lack of heroism renders comic. The Montague Benvolio enters and tries to stop them, but he is himself taunted to fight in earnest with the Capulet Tybalt. The uproar caused by Veronese citizens joining in the fray brings Lord and Lady Capulet and Lord and Lady Montague to the scene and, finally, the Prince of Verona, Escalus, who commands peace and decrees that any further fighting between the two families will be punished by death. When the stage is cleared, Benvolio explains to Montague how the fight began. We then learn of Romeo's strangely solitary habits and depressed mood, which his father, Montague, is unable to understand. As Romeo enters, Benvolio resolves to discover what troubles him. Romeo admits he is sad because the lady he loves does not return his affection. Should he, as Benvolio advises, try to forget her by seeking out other women, their appearance would only impress upon him the more strongly how much the beauty of the woman he loves excels theirs.

NOTES AND GLOSSARY:

bucklers:	small shields
carry coals:	a dirty task performed by the lowest servants, and so a proverbial expression meaning to put up with being humiliated or insulted
colliers:	coal merchants; colloquially a term of abuse because of the low social position of colliers
choler:	anger; a pun on 'collier'
draw:	draw our swords
collar:	hangman's noose; a pun on 'collier' and 'choler'
moved:	aroused, angered
move . . . moved:	Gregory now uses 'move' literally, and so means that in a quarrel Sampson would run, not hold his ground and fight
dog:	worthless fellow
take the wall:	the side of the path next to the building was the best on which to walk to avoid the mess in the gutters and rubbish that might be thrown from the windows above; Sampson is boasting that he would not step aside for any Montague

weakest . . . wall: Gregory turns Sampson's boast against him by using a proverb which again uses 'wall' but means that the less powerful are pushed aside by the stronger

thrust: Sampson continues the witty exchange by applying Gregory's words to women, who are pushed against the wall by their lovers

civil: Sampson is being ironic

maidenhead: virginity

sense: meaning

sense: feeling

fish: women; a slang term

poor-John: hake, a kind of fish, dried and salted; this was eaten by poor people

Fear me not: do not be afraid for me, on my account; in the next line Gregory takes the words in the sense 'do not be afraid *of* me'

marry: an exclamation (from 'By the Virgin Mary'), but no stronger in sense than 'indeed' in modern English

list: please

bite . . . thumb: an insulting gesture such as might provoke a quarrel

for you: ready to fight you

one . . . kinsmen: Gregory, a Capulet servant, must mean Tybalt, though the Montague Benvolio enters first

washing: slashing

art . . . drawn: have you your sword out

heartless hinds: a pun on female deer ('hinds') without their stags ('harts'), meaning cowardly ('heartless') woman servants ('hinds')

manage: use

bills . . . partisans: kinds of pikes

Hold me not: Montague speaks to his wife, as is clear from the next line

profaners: misusers

neighbour-stained: stained with the blood of neighbours

mistempered: wrongly made ('tempered') because you use them in bad temper

airy: vague; this is all we hear of the cause of the quarrel between Capulets and Montagues

cankered . . . peace: grown rusty through lack of use

cankered hate: malignant hate

pay . . . peace: pay the penalty for breaking the peace

pain:	penalty
new abroach:	newly open
by:	near by
withal:	thereby
on . . . part:	on one side or the other
drive:	drove
covert:	concealment
most sought:	wanted above all to be
where . . . not:	where fewest people might
humour:	inclination
who:	him who
augmenting:	adding to
Aurora:	goddess of the dawn
heavy:	sad
pens:	shuts
portentous:	ominous
humour:	mood
importuned:	asked repeatedly and urgently
by any means:	by all means, in every way possible
close:	secretive, reserved
sounding:	fathoming, being understood (literally, 'measured')
envious:	malicious
shrift:	confession
But new:	only just
makes:	would make
view:	appearance; Benvolio thinks of Cupid, god of love
muffled:	Cupid was often depicted with his eyes covered – love is blind
still:	always
create:	created; Romeo, trying in vain to describe his feelings, in frustration calls on 'anything', the first thing that God created from nothing, for example
coz:	cousin
propagate:	increase
discreet:	discriminating
A . . . sweet:	a poison which chokes (the life out of you) and a preserved sweet (which is delicious and desirable)
Soft:	go softly, that is, wait a moment
sadness:	earnest
groan:	Romeo takes 'sadness' in the sense of 'sorrow'
sadly:	seriously
aimed . . . near:	guessed as much
fair:	easily seen; a play on 'fair', meaning 'beautiful', in the preceding line ·

Cupid's arrow:	anyone pierced by an arrow from the bow of the archer Cupid would fall in love
Dian's wit:	Romeo's lady has the cleverness and skill of Diana, goddess of chastity, and so can preserve herself from Romeo's amorous advances
stay:	submit to, endure
ope:	open
store:	wealth
sparing:	refraining, forbearing
starved:	killed
beauties:	beautiful ladies
in question:	to mind
masks:	ladies of rank would wear masks at public festivities
passing:	surpassing, exceptionally
note:	reminder
pay:	pay you for that, that is, Benvolio will teach Romeo to forget
die in debt:	die with payment unmade, die in the attempt

Act I Scene 2

Time: Sunday afternoon (I.1.100; I.2.1–2)

The scene begins with Count Paris, whom we now meet for the first time, asking Capulet for permission to marry his daughter (Juliet). Capulet hesitates, because Juliet is so young, but says he would agree if she consents to be Paris's wife. Inviting Paris to the feast that is to be held that night, Capulet advises him to look at the ladies there to be sure it is Juliet whom he would like to marry. As the servant whom Capulet directs to invite his guests cannot read their names on the list he is given, he asks Romeo, who enters with Benvolio, to read them for him. Rosaline, the lady Romeo loves, is one of the guests: because of this, Romeo and Benvolio decide to go to the feast, although they have not been invited. Benvolio hopes to show Romeo that Rosaline cannot equal the beauty of the other ladies present; Romeo wants simply to see Rosaline. (We should notice that the character of Rosaline plays no part in the play: she is merely mentioned. Shakespeare wants the audience's attention to be focused solely on Romeo and Juliet. To introduce Rosaline and develop Romeo's relationship with her on stage would be to distract the audience from the main love story).

NOTES AND GLOSSARY:

County:	count
bound:	bound to keep the peace

reckoning:	reputation
at odds:	at variance, quarrelling
suit:	wooing, request to marry
hopes:	hopes for the future, that is, children
will . . . consent:	desire for her to agree
is . . . part:	is only part of the matter (Paris has to get Juliet's consent as well)
she agreed:	when once she has agreed
within . . . choice:	according to what she chooses
according:	agreeing
accustomed:	customary, traditional
store:	company
Earth . . . stars:	young ladies so beautiful they seem to be stars that have come down to earth
inherit:	receive
mine:	my daughter (Juliet)
stand . . . number:	count as one of the crowd
though . . . none:	though amongst so many hardly noticeable ('reckoning' meaning 'counting'), and not equal to the others ('reckoning' meaning 'assessment')
sirrah:	a word used by gentlemen to address their inferiors
trudge:	walk (without the sense of weary effort the word has in modern English)
stay:	wait
It . . . nets:	proverbs meaning you should stick to what you know how to do, but the servant, of course, being ignorant, muddles them up: the last belongs to the shoemaker, the yard to the tailor, the net to the fisherman and the pencil to the painter
writ:	written
holp:	helped
with . . . languish:	by making another languish, fade away; Benvolio is trying to persuade Romeo to 'cure' himself of his love for Rosaline by finding another lady to love
plantain:	Romeo takes the 'infection' of line 49 literally, and so wittily suggests a herbal remedy; a plantain is a common English wayside plant which was used both to cure infection and to staunch blood from wounds
broken:	wounded, rather than literally broken
God . . . e'en:	God give you good evening
crush:	drink
Rosaline:	the first time Romeo's beloved is identified
unattainted:	unprejudiced, impartial

these:	these eyes of mine
poised:	balanced, weighed
scant:	scarcely
my own:	my own as belonging to my lady

Act I Scene 3

Time: later on Sunday afternoon (I.3.81)

Constantly interrupted by the Nurse, who cannot stop herself talking, Lady Capulet tells Juliet that Paris wants to marry her, and advises her to take careful note of how handsome he is at the feast that night. Juliet agrees to see if she likes him. In this scene, in which we first meet her, Juliet is submissive .and obedient to her parents (see especially 11.98–100); when she has fallen in love she will discover a new independence of mind.

NOTES AND GLOSSARY:

bade:	bid, told
lamb, ladybird:	words used lovingly to children
God forbid:	that is, God forbid that anything should have happened to her as she does not come
give . . . awhile:	leave us alone for a while
thou's:	thou shalt
counsel:	private talk
pretty:	reasonable, that is, no longer a child
teen:	sorrow
Lammastide:	1 August, a harvest festival
odd:	a few
Susan:	the Nurse's own daughter
wormwood:	a bitter-tasting plant
dug:	nipple; the Nurse suckled Juliet (it was quite common for noble ladies to have 'wet nurses' for their babies); the wormwood was to wean the baby
I . . . brain:	I can remember
fool:	used as a term of affection here
tetchy:	cross
trow:	believe
high-lone:	all alone, by herself
rood:	the cross of Christ
'A:	he
holidam:	holiness; a common exclamation
it:	she
stinted:	stopped

it . . . it:	she . . . her
stone:	testicle
dispositions:	the sense is singular, disposition, inclination
man of wax:	a model, that is, perfect man
married lineament:	harmonious feature (of his face)
one . . . content:	each suits the other, so making a perfect whole
margent:	margin; throughout this speech Lady Capulet compares Paris's face to a book
only lacks:	there is only needed
The . . . hide:	the sense is that just as fish live in the sea so a fair man (Paris) needs a fair wife (Juliet)
endart:	dart, pierce
Nurse cursed:	the Nurse is cursed (for not being there to help)
in extremity:	in dire need of help
wait:	serve at table
straight:	straightaway, immediately

Act I Scene 4

Time: Sunday evening (I.2.20, 81–100; I.3.81)

Romeo, his cousin Benvolio and his friend Mercutio (a kinsman of the Prince (III.1.109, 145, 188–9; V.3.295) whom we now meet for the first time) discuss whether to go into Capulet's feast. Although Benvolio and Romeo have not been invited (Mercutio is included amongst the guests on the servant's list (I.2.64–9)), it was quite usual for uninvited maskers to join such parties, and Benvolio is all for going in. Romeo, however, does not care to dance, and, because of a dream, fears something awful – perhaps even his death – will result if they do go in. But Mercutio makes light of his fears, and they enter. The scene adds little to the action, but it introduces a note of foreboding just as Romeo is to meet Juliet for the first time, and it introduces to us the important character of Mercutio.

NOTES AND GLOSSARY:

maskers:	people wearing masks on their faces; although masked balls (or dances), which were fashionable at this time, should not be confused with *masques,* dramatic entertainments involving music and dancing, such as Ben Jonson composed, improvised masques could easily be presented by people in masks and costumes at such a party as Capulet's (the examples from Shakespeare cited in the following notes illustrate this)

What . . . excuse: shall we introduce ourselves and excuse our intrusion; it was customary for maskers to present themselves, often with a formal speech – see, for example, Shakespeare's *Love's Labour's Lost,* V.2.158–69, and *Henry VIII,* I.4.65–72

The . . . prolixity: such speeches ('prolixity') are out of fashion ('date')

Cupid: maskers would often send a boy, dressed as Cupid, to introduce them – see, for example, Shakespeare's *Timon of Athens,* I.2.117–22

hoodwinked: blindfolded

Tartar's . . . bow: Cupid carried a bow from which to loose his arrows of love: shaped like a lip it was unlike the curved English bow; Shakespeare perhaps thought this was the shape of the bows carried by the Tartar people of central Asia (although it is in fact Grecian) or, more probably, he used the word 'Tartar' vaguely to mean 'Eastern'

lath: thin piece of wood

crowkeeper: scarecrow

without-book: memorised

measure . . . will: judge us as they like

measure . . . measure: dance one dance for them

torch: torchbearers would not join in the dancing

ambling: dancing (a contemptuous term)

So: which so

stakes: ties, fixes; bears were tied to a stake (or post) in the ground for the sport of bear-baiting

bound: tied

bound: leap

pitch: height

case: mask

visage: face

visor . . . visor: mask for an ugly face

quote: notice

betake . . . legs: that is, in dancing

rushes: these would be strewn on the floor

proverbed . . . phrase: supported (in what I wish to do) by an old proverb; Romeo thinks of the proverb that the onlooker sees the best of the game

game: that is, here, dancing

ne'er so fair: never so good (as now); there was a proverbial saying that one should leave the game (gambling) when the game was at its best

done: finish with

dun's . . . mouse: a quibble on 'done' in line 39; because the mouse is dark ('dun') it is not easily seen, and so, the meaning is 'be quiet', and so unnoticed like the mouse

constable's . . . word: the constable, or policeman, would bid his companions be quiet when he is waiting to catch a criminal

Dun: a name for a horse; there was an expression 'Dun in the mire', like the modern 'stick-in-the-mud', someone who will not venture on anything new

burn daylight: waste time; Romeo takes Mercutio literally in the next line

Take . . . meaning: take the sense of what I say, don't take me literally

for . . . wits: for good sense is five times more apparent in what we mean than in what we say (that is, than in the words which are the result of what we learn through our five senses)

tonight: last night

in . . . asleep: in line 51 Mercutio used 'lie' in the sense 'tell an untruth'; Romeo takes it in the sense 'lie down'

Queen Mab: queen of the fairies

agate: a precious stone, often engraved and set in rings

atomies: tiny creatures

grub: insect that bores holes into fruit (in this case, nuts)

spinners: spiders

traces: reins

film: fine thread of cobweb

Pricked . . . maid: there was a saying that when maids were idle worms grew in their fingers

suit: petition (which a courtier would present to the king for a fee)

tithe-pig: a pig due to the parish priest who received the tenth part (or 'tithe') of the agricultural produce of the people who lived in his parish

benefice: position in the church held by a parish priest, for which he received payment

ambuscadoes: ambushes

Spanish blades: Spain was famous for the quality of its swords

healths: drinks (from the expression 'drink to your health')

bakes: matts, tangles together in a hard lump

elf-locks: tangled hair was thought to be the work of elves; to untangle it would bring bad luck (line 91)

sluttish:	very dirty
hag;	wicked, ugly fairy
learns . . . bear:	teaches them first how to bear children; Mercutio in fact means 'teach them how to conceive children' for he is thinking of young women dreaming of sex as a result of Mab's influence
carriage:	both 'deportment' and 'the carrying of a child in the womb'
from ourselves:	from our purpose
date:	time
expire . . . term:	complete the allotted span
steerage:	guidance

Act I Scene 5

Time: Sunday evening (I.2.20, 81–100; I.3.81)

In Capulet's house the servants are busy clearing the hall for the dance which is to follow the meal. Capulet welcomes the maskers and watches the dance, recollecting with his cousin his own dancing days long ago. Tybalt realises that one of the maskers is a Montague, and is furious at the intrusion. Capulet, identifying Romeo, orders Tybalt to control himself and behave civilly to so fine a youth, but Tybalt resolves that this will not be the end of the matter. Romeo, who does not take part in the dance, has noticed Juliet and is overpowered by her beauty. He approaches her when the dance ends and in the fourteen lines of an English sonnet he woos her, they fall in love and kiss. The Nurse interrupts them, and the scene ends with Romeo learning that Juliet is a Capulet, she that Romeo is a Montague – that is, that each loves an enemy. Thus, this first meeting of the lovers ends on a note of foreboding.

NOTES AND GLOSSARY:

take away:	clear away
trencher:	wooden plate
joint-stools:	wooden stools
court-cupboard:	sideboard
marchpane:	marzipan
let . . . Nell:	the servants are to have their own party; Susan and Nell would be their guests
the . . . all:	a cheery saying, dismissing present worries in the remark that it will make no difference when we are dead (the 'longer liver', Death, will take us all, so we might as well be merry now)

corns:	patches of hard, painful skin caused by ill-fitting shoes
walk about:	have a dance
makes dainty:	is coy (in refusing to dance for no very good reason)
Am . . . ye:	does what I say affect you
A hall:	clear the room, let us have a hall
knaves:	the servants (the word is used in good humour here)
turn . . . up:	in order to clear the room for dancing .
unlooked-for:	because Romeo and his friends were not expected
Pentecost:	Whitsun, an annual Christian festival commemorating the coming of the Holy Spirit to the Apostles
ward:	youth under twenty-one years of age
Ethiop:	Ethiopian, strictly, though the word was used of any Negro
shows:	appears
The . . . done:	when the dance has ended
rude:	rough
should:	must
slave:	not literally, but a term of contempt
antic face:	fantastic or grotesque mask
fleer:	sneer
solemnity:	celebration
stock:	parentage, the noble line of a family's descent
portly:	dignified
well-governed:	well mannered
patient:	calm (Capulet does *not* mean that Tybalt should be patient and wait for another opportunity)
ill . . . semblance:	unsuitable appearance
goodman:	a term used to address some one below the rank of gentleman (yeoman) and so an insult to Tybalt
Go to:	an expression of exasperation
mutiny:	disturbance
You . . . hoop:	a colloquial expression explained by Capulet's following ironic 'You'll be the man!'
saucy:	insolent (the word was then stronger in sense than in modern English)
contrary:	contradict
hearts:	friends (Capulet turns aside to address his guests)
perforce:	by force, forcibly
wilful:	eager, determined
seeming:	apparently
If . . . take:	in these lines, which make up a sonnet, Shakespeare

pursues an elaborate religious conceit (or extended image), likening Romeo's approach to Juliet to that of a pilgrim to the shrine of a saint; such use of religious imagery was not unusual in love poetry, but the delicate ingenuity and detail of this example are remarkable; it has added point in that Romeo's name means, in Italian, 'pilgrim to Rome'

shrine: that is, Juliet's hand

mannerly: proper

palmer: a pilgrim who carried a palm leaf to show he had been to Jerusalem; here, of course, the word is also a play on the palm of the hand

though . . . sake: though they grant what is prayed for, that is, they are 'moved' (persuaded) by prayers, though they do not move physically

by . . . book: Juliet either admits she is deeply affected by the kiss, or she draws back and covers her feelings, for the phrase may mean either 'expertly' ('you have learned how') or 'formally' ('you kiss as though following written instructions, without feeling')

chinks: money (because Juliet is the Capulet heir)

dear account: awful reckoning to pay

my . . . debt: indebted to, dependent on, my foe

banquet: not the main meal, which was cleared away for the dance, but a light supper

fay: faith

waxes: grows

Prodigious: ominous, monstrous

Act II Scene 1

Time: Sunday night, immediately after Capulet's party (II.1.3–4)

After the Chorus has summarised the situation, stressing the fact that Romeo and Juliet cannot easily meet because of their families' feud, Romeo enters for a moment, and we hear that he cannot bear to leave the house where Juliet lives. He withdraws as Benvolio and Mercutio enter looking for him. Benvolio thinks he has seen Romeo jump over a wall (which, we learn in II.2, surrounds the Capulet house and garden) and Mercutio attempts to recall him by making fun of, and bawdy remarks about, Romeo's love for Rosaline. Mercutio, of course, does not know Romeo no longer loves Rosaline, and he expects that his unflattering jests at the expense of Romeo's great love will so annoy Romeo that he will be provoked to rejoin them. But Romeo does not return and the two friends go home to bed without him.

NOTES AND GLOSSARY:

Chorus: it is difficult to see why the Chorus's speech (unremarkable poetically) is needed, since it adds nothing to our understanding of the action; it is now usually omitted in performances

old desire: that is, Romeo's love for Rosaline

young affection: that is, Romeo's new love for Juliet

fair: fair woman (Rosaline)

matched: compared

supposed: Juliet is supposed to be Romeo's enemy as she is a Capulet, but she is not really as he loves her

use to: are accustomed to

Tempering extremities: modifying extremely harsh circumstances (by the meetings we are about to see in later scenes)

go forward: that is, go forward beyond Juliet's house

dull earth: Romeo's own body (God created Adam from earth)

centre: three senses combine here: (*i*) earth was thought to be a heavy element which tended down to the centre of the world (because of gravitation, though that was not then understood), and so Romeo, as earth, must go to his centre; (*ii*) the centre of Romeo's world is Juliet, as she is all to him; (*iii*) the heart is the centre of man, and, as Juliet has Romeo's heart, he must return to her to find his centre: the sense of all these meanings is that Romeo cannot leave Juliet, the centre of his life

orchard: probably garden, rather than literally an orchard (though this one does have fruit trees in it, see II.2.108)

conjure: to call up spirits by reciting magic words (Mercutio goes on to make fun of Romeo's love by reciting a mock incantation to him)

Abraham Cupid: two senses are possible: (*i*) the cunning and roguish Cupid, naked but for a loin cloth, is like the 'Abraham men', half-naked beggars and thieves who wandered England – so, 'rascally Cupid'; (*ii*) the patriarch Abraham in the Old Testament lived to be 175 years old, and Cupid, though a child, was an old god – so 'old Cupid'

gossip Venus:	familiar friend Venus, the goddess of love and mother of Cupid, who has already been mentioned many times and is referred to again in the next line
purblind:	blind
trim:	accurately
King Cophetua:	the hero of an old ballad who fell in love with a beggar girl; the point of the allusion is that this was an unlikely match, and so Cupid was particularly clever to bring it about
ape . . . dead:	a term of affection; Mercutio means that as Romeo pretends to be dead by not appearing, his ghost must be conjured up
demesnes:	domains, that is, Rosaline's sexual parts
raise:	conjure up
circle:	conjurors worked in a magic circle, but here, and in 'raise', 'stand' and 'laid', there is a second bawdy sense, as these words all refer to the sexual act
invocation:	summoning
consorted:	accompanied
humourous:	humid and (with reference to Romeo's apparent unfriendliness) moody
medlar:	a fruit, and a pun on 'meddle', meaning 'to make love'
as . . . medlars:	'medlar' was used to refer to a woman's sexual parts
open-arse:	dialect name for medlar, and a reference to the female body
poppering pear:	a kind of pear and a pun on the act of love-making
truckle bed:	a small bed, such as a child might use; Mercutio is pretending to be young and innocent – he is going to his bed, leaving Romeo to the sexual activities Mercutio has been attributing to him

---

Act II Scene 2

Time: Sunday night, immediately following II.1 (II.2.1), *to dawn on Monday* (II.2.176, 188–91)

The love theme of the first part of the play now begins to move quickly to its climax. Although Romeo and Juliet have only just met, by the time the crucial meeting we now see is over, they are planning to marry. It is, indeed, for the remarkably beautiful treatment of the confession of love in this scene that the play is best remembered and loved. As the scene opens, Romeo dismisses Mercutio's jokes, and, seeing Juliet at her balcony, adores her beauty. Juliet, not knowing Romeo is below, confesses that she loves him despite the fact that he is a Montague. Romeo speaks to her and, although Juliet is afraid for his life, he remains in the garden and they admit their love. Juliet speaks honestly and frankly of her affection, and freely tells Romeo that if he means what he says and can send word the next day how they may be married, she will readily be his wife. She arranges to send a go-between to Romeo by nine in the morning to learn what plan he has made. When she goes in, Romeo decides to go to see his father confessor, Friar Laurence, for advice on how to bring about the marriage.

NOTES AND GLOSSARY:

He . . . wound:	someone who has never been hurt makes light of another's scars: Romeo means by the proverb that as Mercutio has never been in love he can easily laugh at a lover's sorrows; the saying is apt since lovers were often said to be 'wounded' by love since they had been pierced by Cupid's arrow
be . . . maid:	Romeo has likened Juliet to the sun; in not wanting her to be the maid of the virgin goddess of the moon, Diana, he is saying that he hopes she may accept his love and so cease to be a virgin
vestal:	virgin
livery:	costume
fools:	that is, those who remain virgin and unmarried
spheres:	in the old astronomy of Ptolemy the stars and planets were thought to revolve around the earth as though in round, transparent tubes, called 'spheres'
they:	that is, the stars
wherefore:	why; that is, why are you Romeo and a Montague and not a member of some other family?
refuse:	reject
though not:	even if you were not
owes:	owns
doff:	take off
bescreened:	hidden
thee dislike:	offends, displeases, you
the place death:	that you are in this place will result in your death
o'erperch:	fly over
that dares love:	that love dares to

peril:	power (to harm, if she refuses him), danger
proof:	protected, immune
but thou:	unless you, if you do not
prorogued:	put off until later
wanting of:	if I lacked
counsel:	advice
Fain . . . form:	gladly would I follow custom, that is, by denying her love, the retort that would be expected from a lady addressed by her lover
compliment:	conventional polite manners, formality: Juliet's determination here to speak plainly of her love, though hardly what would be expected of a young girl alone at night with a man, is the key to her whole character; it contrasts very obviously with Romeo's elaborate imagery – notice how Juliet interrupts him at 1.109
perjuries:	lies
Jove:	king of the gods in Roman mythology
faithfully:	honestly, truly
So . . . wilt:	if that will make you
fond:	affectionate and foolish
cunning . . . strange:	skill to be aloof or distant, that is, to follow the usual rules of courtship
not:	do not
discovered:	uncovered, revealed
orb:	orbit
unadvised:	unconsidered
as that:	as that which is
frank:	generous
bent:	intention, inclination
thee my lord:	thee as my lord
strife:	striving
Love . . . love:	a loved one . . . a loved one
toward school:	like schoolboys going to school
tassel-gentle:	tercel-gentle, a male falcon, the most prized by falconers (and so a compliment to Romeo)
Bondage . . . hoarse:	as a young girl Juliet would not be free to leave the house unaccompanied or to meet a man without a chaperon; hence, as a lover, she is 'bound' and cannot call out to Romeo for fear of discovery
Echo:	a mythical nymph condemned to repeat the last words any one spoke to her, who, unable to declare her love for Narcissus, lived alone in a cave until

	she died of a broken heart, leaving only her voice behind
nyas:	a young hawk which has not yet left the nest to fly (and so Romeo's fitting reply to 'tassel-gentle')
remembering:	while I reflect on
wanton:	mischievous child
gyves:	shackles
fleckled:	dappled, spotted
Titan's wheels:	according to Greek mythology the Titans were the first gods; the Titan sun god Hyperion rode across the sky in a chariot
ghostly:	spiritual
close:	either confined, small, or concealed, secret
dear hap:	dear happening, that is, good fortune

Act II Scene 3

Time: early Monday morning, immediately following II.2 (II.2.188–93; II.3.1–4, 28–30, 38)

Romeo visits Friar Laurence, as he had decided to do at the end of II.2. The Friar's long soliloquy, with which the scene opens, serves to introduce him to the audience as a kindly and good-natured man and one who is skilled with the poison and medicine that may be made from plants. We are thus prepared to accept that he could make the potion he later gives to Juliet. More than this, the Friar's vision of the world as potentially good and evil underlines one of the main themes of the play: love and hate are very close, as poison and medicine may be derived from one plant, and should hate predominate, love will be destroyed. Some texts bring Romeo in at line 19, so that he overhears the last part of the speech: it is certainly true that the final lines of the speech are an unintentional prophecy of Romeo's fate, for he will die of poison because of the circumstances the hatred of Montagues and Capulets has brought about.

The Friar is glad to hear Romeo is no longer infatuated with Rosaline, but astonished to learn that another lady has taken her place. Nevertheless, he agrees to help arrange the marriage, as this may serve to unite the families of Montague and Capulet. Although this is merely mentioned at the end of the scene, it should be carefully noted, as it is the only justification for the Friar's willingness to assist in a secret marriage. Furthermore, it means that he, too, like the Prince, Escalus, is anxious to end the feud. With the Church (the Friar) and the State (the Prince) both trying to heal old wounds, it is the more

tragic that the love of Romeo and Juliet should be destroyed by this
very quarrel and that only their deaths bring about the reconciliation
which the Friar hopes here their marriage will achieve.

NOTES AND GLOSSARY:

advance:	raise
osier cage:	willow basket
baleful:	poisonous
What:	that which
that:	that too
children:	that is, the plants
divers:	many different
None . . . some:	there is no plant which does not have some good qualities
mickle:	great
stones:	rocks, in the sense of 'minerals'
naught:	none, that is, no created thing
to the earth:	that is, to the inhabitants of the earth
aught:	any, that is, any created thing
strained:	forced away, perverted
Revolts . . . abuse:	turns away from its true nature if it happens to be abused
medicine:	medicinal, curative
with . . . part:	by means of that part (the nose, which smells the plant) revives ('cheers') the other parts of the body
stays:	stops
And . . . plant:	the Friar here compares the spiritual state of man to the natural state of plants as he has described it: as poison and medicine are found in one plant, so man has good and evil in him ('grace and rude will'); if the evil ('the worser') predominates, then the man is consumed by wickedness and spiritual death ('the canker death') overtakes him
canker:	canker worm, a caterpillar that eats plants
Good morrow:	good morning
Benedicite:	(*Latin*) 'May you be blessed'
argues . . . head:	shows a disturbed mind
So soon:	that you so soon
good morrow:	goodbye
unbruised:	unharmed by the world, that is, innocent
unstuffed:	not filled with troubles
distemperature:	uneasiness of mind
one . . . wounded:	that is, I fell in love with one who loves me; the image derives from the idea of being shot with one

of Cupid's arrows, though it is especially appropriate here as Juliet is Romeo's 'enemy'

I . . . hatred:	that is, such as might be expected if one has been wounded by an enemy
intercession:	petition, request (a word with religious overtones)
steads:	helps
homely:	unsophisticated, that is, plain, straightforward
pass:	go along
Holy . . . Francis:	as a Franciscan Friar, Laurence exclaims by the name of the saint who founded his religious order
Jesu Maria:	Jesus son of Mary
sallow:	pale
sentence:	saying, maxim
Thy . . . spell:	your expressions of love were as though recited ('read') by memory ('rote') by some one who could not understand ('spell') what he had learned to say; these comments point to the conventional and very ornate language Romeo has used to describe his feelings; unlike Juliet, who speaks plainly, as the Friar would wish, Romeo has always used the literary terms and images of love poetry
In . . . respect:	because of one thing
may . . . prove:	may prove so fortunate as
stand one:	insist on, or, depend on

Act II Scene 4

Time: 12 noon on Monday (II.4.110)

Benvolio and Mercutio, who went home to bed at the end of II.1 without finding Romeo, are still looking for him the next morning. We hear from them that Tybalt has carried out his threat (I.5.91–2) not to ignore the matter of Romeo's intrusion into Capulet's party and has sent a challenge to Montague, which Benvolio believes Romeo will accept. Here is the first, ominous, suggestion of a threat to the love which has developed in the previous scenes. Notice that Shakespeare introduces it before Romeo and Juliet have been married: he wants to ensure that although things are apparently going well for the two lovers, there is a slight sense of unease in the back of the audience's mind, a lurking fear that things are not really going as well as they seem. Because of this, even as we watch the lovers preparing to marry, we cannot escape the feeling that the happiness they expect will not be the result.

When Romeo enters (coming from his meeting with the Friar) he is in good spirits (for the first time in the play) and engages in witty exchanges with Mercutio. In II.2.167–9 Juliet had arranged to send a messenger to Romeo, and now the Nurse comes. Romeo tells her to arrange for Juliet to go to confession that afternoon and says they will then be married by the Friar. He also arranges for his servant to give the Nurse a rope ladder, by means of which he will enter Juliet's room that night. The Nurse agrees to these plans.

NOTES AND GLOSSARY:

should: can

man: servant

answer: accept the challenge, though Mercutio jokingly takes it in its usual sense in the next line

how he dares: saying that he dares to fight

already dead: that is, through the sufferings of love

pin: centre

blind . . . boy: Cupid

butt-shaft: blunt arrow

Prince of Cats: Tybalt's name was given to the cat in the old medieval story of Reynard the Fox

compliments: formal courtesies

He . . . hay: Mercutio makes fun of Tybalt's valour by ridiculing him as skilled with the slender, pointed Italian rapier, which does not cut but pierces the opponent; duels with such weapons only became fashionable in England in the 1590s, and were scorned by those who preferred the heavier English sword, with an edge which cut the opponent; Mercutio sees the Italian duel as a matter of elaborate formality and not a serious fight

as . . . pricksong: as you sing carefully following printed music, that is, according to the rules

rests . . . rests: observes every detail of the music

butcher . . . button: because the rapier hits only a small point and does not cause a great wound like a sword

duellist: the first use of the word in English literature; Mercutio uses it in scorn

first house: finest school of duelling

cause . . . *hay*: these are all duelling terms

The pox of: a plague on

antic: grotesque

affecting: affected

fantasticoes: fops

new tuners:	followers of every new fashion, who affect the latest idioms and forms of speech (Mercutio goes on to give examples)
tall:	brave
fashion-mongers:	people who study and follow every new fashion
pardon-me:	a new and over-used phrase among courtiers of the time (in Mercutio's view, a hypocritical phrase)
who . . . bench:	Mercutio's usual wordplay: who insist ('stand') so much on the new code of manners ('form') that they cannot tolerate ('sit') the old ways ('bench')
roe:	several senses are combined: (*i*) the spawn of a fish, so 'unmanned'; (*ii*) a kind of deer, so 'without his dear one'; (*iii*) first syllable of Romeo's name, and so 'only half himself'
numbers:	verses
Petrarch . . . Laura:	the famous medieval Italian poet Petrarch wrote of his love for Laura, and established many of those literary conventions and images which Elizabethan poets (and Romeo!) still used
Dido . . . Thisbe:	all famous women and lovers celebrated in Classical literature; that all their love affairs ended tragically strikes an ominous note
hildings:	worthless women
slop:	loose trousers (Romeo, of course, has not been to bed, and so has not changed since the party)
gave . . . counterfeit:	deceived us
bow . . . hams:	Mercutio takes 'courtesy' in line 49 as 'curtsey', and suggests Romeo spent the night bending his legs in lovemaking to Rosaline
Meaning . . . goose:	now that he has arranged the marriage Romeo is in much better spirits and, for the first time in the play, is Mercutio's equal in wit: in these exchanges they play a number of word games: (*i*) courtesy, curtsey, courteous (lines 53–6); (*ii*) pink ('perfection', a flower and an ornament on a shoe, lines 56–9); (*iii*) pump (a shoe), sole (of a shoe), solely singular (uniquely remarkable), single-soled (weak), solely (only) and singleness (silliness, lines 59–65); (*iv*) wild goose-chase (a horse race in which all follow the leader, and so, a pointless chase), wild-goose (silly person), goose (prostitute and jester), cooked goose that needs sweeting (apple sauce) and broad goose (rude jester, lines 70–85)

Swits:	switch, riding crop or whip
cheverel:	kind of leather that stretches easily
ell:	measure of forty-five inches
natural:	idiot
bauble:	decorated stick, and a bawdy expression for penis
occupy . . . argument:	deal with the subject
gear:	matter
a sail:	Romeo means that he sees some one coming, as the look-out on a ship would cry 'a sail' when he sighted another ship
shirt . . . smock:	a man and a woman
prick:	point, but the clock-hand is 'bawdy' because 'prick' also means 'penis'
noon:	Juliet's go-between was supposed to arrive by 9 a.m. (II.2.167–9), and Juliet had sent the Nurse on time (II.5.1); she has obviously been distracted from her purpose – that she should be late is entirely consistent with the character we know from what she says on stage
can . . . Romeo:	a rather strange question, since she had met Romeo the night before at the party (I.5.112–18, 134–6); such disregard for accuracy in all details is characteristic of Shakespeare
for . . . worse:	Romeo turns round the usual sense, 'for want of a better', to say 'since there is no worse'
confidence:	confidential, private conversation
endite:	invite
bawd:	woman who keeps a brothel
hare:	slang for a prostitute
lenten pie:	as no meat was supposed to be eaten during the period of Lent (the forty days before Easter), a hare pie would go stale
hoar:	mouldy, and a pun on 'whore'
merchant:	fellow (a term of derision)
ropery:	naughty jokes
stand to:	maintain, carry out
Jacks:	insolent fellows
Scurvy:	worthless, contemptible
flirt-gills:	loose, immoral women
skains-mates:	villainous companions
suffer:	allow
lead . . . paradise:	deceive her, that is, seduce her by falsely promising to marry her
gross:	monstrous

weak:	contemptible
tackled stair:	rope ladder
topgallant:	summit
convoy:	conveyance
trusty:	faithful
quit . . . pains:	reward your efforts
Two . . . away:	a proverb meaning that two can keep a secret, but not three
Warrant:	I warrant, assure, promise
prating:	chattering
lay . . . aboard:	a saying meaning 'to lay claim to'
had as lief:	would as willingly
versal:	universal, whole
dog's name:	because when pronounced 'R' sounds like a dog's growl
sententious:	the Nurse (who quite often misuses words) means 'sentence', a saying
apace:	quickly

Act II Scene 5

Time: early Monday afternoon, immediately following II.4 (II.4.110; II.5.1–11)

Juliet waits impatiently and anxiously for the return of the Nurse, who has been gone for three hours. When the Nurse does return, it is only after repeated questions that Juliet learns that Romeo has arranged the marriage for that afternoon. This short scene shows how Shakespeare can achieve dramatic effect from the most unlikely material. Romeo's message has to be conveyed to Juliet, but, instead of hearing it delivered immediately, we are made to wait, our impatience and frustration growing with Juliet's as the Nurse continues to complain of her tiredness instead of telling what Romeo said. The simple delivery of a message thus involves us in sympathy with Juliet, irritation and amusement at the Nurse, and relief when the plan is finally made known. That the scene ends with Juliet speaking of 'high fortune' is ominous: in tragedy, it is when the hero is at the height of his fortune that he is mostly likely to fall.

NOTES AND GLOSSARY:

Perchance:	perhaps
That's . . . so:	That cannot be
glides:	glide
louring:	dark

nimble pinioned:	swift-winged
draw love:	pull the chariot of the goddess of love, Venus
bandy:	send
And . . . me:	and his words would send her back to me
feign . . . dead:	seem to be dead (because they move so slowly)
leave:	peace
jaunce:	jaunt, walk
stay the circumstance:	wait for the details
simple:	silly
Go . . . God:	get on with you, be about your business
beshrew:	shame on
hot:	impatient, passionate
Marry . . . trow:	a common exclamation; the Nurse pretends to be offended by Juliet's lack of interest in her aches and pains
coil:	bother
hie:	hurry
wanton:	uncontrolled, unrestrained, unmanageable (there is a suggestion of 'passionate' or 'lustful' in the word)
bird's nest:	that is, Juliet's room
drudge:	a servant who has to work hard at mean tasks

Act II Scene 6

Time: later Monday afternoon (II.4.176–82; II.5.66–9)

In an unexpectedly quiet climax to the first movement of the play Romeo and Juliet meet at the Friar's cell and go in to be married. By not presenting the marriage on stage, Shakespeare ensures that the memorable scenes will be the lovers' declaration of love (II.2) and their deaths (V.3). Thus, he gives a starkly simple design to the play. Our experience of it in the theatre is of sudden love and sudden death. The marriage seems, and is made by Shakespeare to seem, almost unimportant beside the love itself; Romeo and Juliet *are* married in the deepest sense – we might almost say that, poetically, the wedding occurred in II.2 when two loving souls met and recognised each other. The formal marriage is but an inevitable consequence of that. Furthermore, by ending this movement of the play so quietly, Shakespeare achieves an obvious contrast with the violence that follows in the next scene: the idyllic, quiet, secret world of love is shattered by Tybalt. The Friar's opening words are cruelly ironic in view of what does happen later, and his words at lines 9–11 tragically prophetic.

NOTES AND GLOSSARY:

So . . . act:	let the heavens so approve, or bless, this holy act
what . . . can:	whatever sorrow can come
countervail:	equal, counterbalance
in . . . deliciousness:	because it is so delicious
confounds:	destroys
tardy:	late
Will . . . flint:	Juliet walks so lightly her feet seem hardly to touch the ground and so will not wear out the rock ('flint')
gossamers:	cobwebs
idles:	drift
vanity:	the pleasures of the world; the Friar for a moment sadly remembers that, from the point of view of religion, such love is insubstantial
As . . . much:	Romeo's 'thanks' for Juliet's 'good evening' to the Friar (probably a kiss) will be too great a return for a single greeting and so she must include Romeo in it ('as much to him')
and that:	and since
blazon:	proclaim, set forth in fine colours
either:	each other
Conceit:	imagination: it is worthy of note that the plain-speaking Juliet refuses Romeo's invitation to 'blazon' their love in fine phrases
I . . . wealth:	I cannot add up ('sum') the total of half my wealth

---

Act III Scene 1

Time: Monday afternoon, an hour after Romeo's marriage (III.1.112–3)

Mercutio and Benvolio are walking in Verona. Mercutio rejects Benvolio's suggestion that they should leave the streets as the Capulets are also out-of-doors and playfully mocks Benvolio's attempt to prevent any fighting by characterising him as extraordinarily quarrelsome. As we see in a moment, Mercutio is in fact describing his own character, for they soon meet Tybalt and Mercutio deliberately provokes him. Tybalt, however, is looking for Romeo, and, when he enters, Tybalt turns to him and insults him. We know that Tybalt is infuriated by Romeo's intrusion at Capulet's party, but to Romeo, newly married to Tybalt's cousin Juliet (and so now related to Tybalt himself), there seems to be no good reason to quarrel. Mercutio is dismayed by what he takes to be Romeo's cowardice in refusing to fight, and he himself draws his sword on Tybalt. As Romeo tries to stop them fighting, Mercutio is fatally wounded by Tybalt. In a moment of grim foresight, Romeo sees that this death will cause much sorrow in days to come, but, nevertheless, to avenge his friend's death, he fights and kills Tybalt. Benvolio persuades Romeo to flee, since the Prince has decreed that anyone guilty of further fighting will be punished by death (I.1.96–7). However, because Tybalt has himself committed a murder, the Prince does not order Romeo's execution, but exiles him from Verona.

Thus, in the scene immediately following his marriage, Romeo is driven from Verona and from Juliet. Throughout the second act his fortunes have been steadily improving: he and Juliet exchanged vows in II.2; in II.3 the Friar agreed to marry them; in II.4 Romeo was in high spirits and told the Nurse of his plan; and in II.6 the marriage was accomplished. Now, in a moment, the movement towards tragedy (of which we had hints in I.4.106–111; I.5.91–2; II.4.6–9, and for which the Chorus has prepared us) begins. It is sadly ironic that Romeo himself does his best to prevent it: it is the misguided sense of honour of his friend, Mercutio, which brings it about.

NOTES AND GLOSSARY:

Capels:	Capulets
operation:	effect
drawer:	waiter
hot:	impetuous
moved . . . moody:	inclined to anger
moody . . . moved:	angry at being incited
two:	Mercutio's wordplay on Benvolio's 'to' in line 14
meat:	flesh
addle . . . egg:	bad as a rotten egg
doublet:	jacket
riband:	ribbon
tutor me:	instruct me against
fee simple:	full title
for . . . quarter:	before an hour and a quarter had passed; Benvolio means that were he as quarrelsome as Mercutio he would be killed in a fight within this time; it is dramatically ironic that Mercutio *will* be killed within this time because of his quarrelsomeness
comes:	come
And but:	only
Consort . . . minstrels:	Tybalt in line 44 meant 'associate with' by 'consortest', but a company of musicians was called a 'consort' and Mercutio sees this as an opportunity to take offence since 'minstrel' (a hired musician) was a term of abuse

fiddlestick:	that is, his sword
Zounds:	an exclamation, from 'By God's wounds'
my man:	the man I am looking for
livery:	Mercutio, still looking for grievances, takes 'man' in line 55 as 'servant' and exclaims that Romeo does not wear the uniform ('livery') of one of Tybalt's hired men
worship:	honour; a polite form of address here used ironically by Mercutio, who means that Romeo is Tybalt's servant, or follower, only in the sense that he will follow him to the place for a duel ('field')
excuse . . . rage:	excuse me from showing the appropriate rage
devise:	guess
tender:	value
Alla stoccata:	a duelling term which Mercutio sarcastically uses as a name for Tybalt
nine lives:	proverbially, a cat has nine lives
as . . . me:	depending on how you treat me
dry-beat:	cudgel, beat without drawing blood
pilcher:	scabbard
bandying:	fighting
sped:	slain
villain:	a term of address to a servant, not here implying bad qualities, as it does in Tybalt's use to the gentleman Romeo in line 60
grave man:	a serious man and a man in a grave; an appropriate, and moving, jest from the dying Mercutio, who has not once been serious in the play
peppered:	killed
book of arthmetic:	book of rules
worms' mean:	that is, a corpse, which the worms will eat
ally:	relative
In:	on
cousin:	relative, through his marriage to Juliet
temper:	character
aspired:	risen to
on more . . . depend:	portends ill fortune on more days to come: this, and the following line, marked out as a couplet, signal the beginning of the tragedy
respective lenity:	leniency or mildness which is respectful (to Tybalt, as Juliet's, and now, Romeo's, relative)
conduct:	conductor, guide
This:	that is, Romeo's sword
Up:	come on

amazed:	bewildered, dazed (a stronger word in Elizabethan English than it is now)
charge:	command
discover:	reveal
unlucky manage:	unfortunate handling
true:	faithful to your word
spoke him fair:	spoke politely to him
nice:	petty, trivial
urged . . . displeasure:	that is, tried to dissuade Tybalt from fighting by reminding him of the Prince's decree against feuding: Benvolio biases his account in Romeo's favour for, although Romeo did 'speak Tybalt fair', he had not mentioned the Prince's displeasure; there is thus some truth in Lady Capulet's later remark, lines 176–7
unruly spleen:	ungovernable bad temper
deaf:	who was deaf: notice that Benvolio does not mention that Mercutio deliberately provoked Tybalt
but that:	so that
retorts:	returns
envious:	hostile
newly entertained:	only just thought of
His . . . end:	in killing Tybalt Romeo had only anticipated the law, which would have condemned Tybalt to death for murdering Mercutio
My blood:	the blood of my family (as Mercutio was his relative)
amerce:	punish by a fine
mine:	my relative
purchase out:	buy off, obliterate
attend our will:	do as I command
Mercy . . . kill:	if the law is merciful to murderers then it simply encourages further murders

---

Act III Scene 2

Time: later Monday afternoon, three hours after the marriage (III.2.99) *and two hours after Romeo's fight* (III.1.112–13)

Juliet is waiting impatiently for the night, which will bring Romeo to her (as he had planned before their marriage II.4.183–7; II.5.72–4). Even as Juliet speaks, however, we know that what is, in effect, her wedding hymn will lead to no such happiness as she anticipates, for we have heard that Romeo is banished. In a strikingly dramatic moment, this news is brought to Juliet. Just as she is taken up with joyful thoughts of Romeo and the consummation of their love, the Nurse enters to dash all her hopes by telling her of Tybalt's death and Romeo's banishment. (A very similar technique is used by Shakespeare at the beginning of V.1.) To the Nurse's surprise, after a moment's shock at what Romeo has done, Juliet is not appalled that he has killed her cousin Tybalt, but full of grief at his banishment. She realises that their wedding night is now to be their farewell, and, in speaking metaphorically of this parting as her death, she darkens the atmosphere of the play and, unknowingly, alerts the audience to her fate. The scene ends with the Nurse agreeing to bring Romeo from Friar Laurence's cell, where he has hidden since the fight.

NOTES AND GLOSSARY:

fiery . . . steeds: the horses which pulled the chariot of the Olympian sun god, Phoebus; in Greek mythology the Olympian gods, of whom Zeus was chief, succeeded the Titans

Phoebus' lodging: the night's resting-place of the sun god, that is, Juliet wants the sun to set below the horizon

waggoner . . . Phaeton: Phaeton was Phoebus's son, whom Phoebus once allowed to drive his chariot with disastrous results for, unable to prevent the chariot racing too near to the earth, Phaeton was destroyed by a thunderbolt from Zeus lest the world be consumed by fire

close: enclosing, concealing

runaway's: who it is that is a 'runaway' is not clear, but the sense is that the lovers will be safe in the darkness, free from spies

civil: decorous, gentle

sober-suited: clothed in sombre colours

lose . . . match: Juliet must yield her body to Romeo ('lose') and so win a husband

hood . . . blood: Juliet is asking the night to hide ('hood') her blushes ('blood') as she yields her virginity, but the image, from falconry, is appropriate in other ways: the head of an untrained ('unmanned') falcon was covered with a hood until it grew used to its owner (or 'man'); Juliet is untrained in the ways of love-making and 'unmanned' because she has not yet had a man as a lover

bating: fluttering

garish:	bright, gaudy
cords:	ropes (that Romeo had given her, II.4.183–7)
weraday:	alas
undone:	ruined
envious:	full of hostility, malicious
Romeo can:	the Nurse means that Romeo can be so full of hostility as to kill Tybalt
cockatrice:	a basilisk, a mythical beast which could kill with a glance
Or those . . . Ay:	if you must answer 'yes' because those eyes (that is, Romeo's) are shut (that is, he is dead)
God . . . mark:	an apologetic exclamation, perhaps because the Nurse points to her own breast
corse:	corpse
bedaubed:	covered
swounded:	swooned
Vile earth:	that is, her own body
heavy:	literally, and meaning 'sad'
bier:	stretcher for carrying a corpse
so contrary:	in such opposite directions (Juliet thought the Nurse had been describing Romeo's body)
dreadful trumpet:	in Christian belief the Day of Judgement (Doomsday) will be announced by the sound of a trumpet
serpent:	when the Devil tempted Eve in Paradise he appeared as a snake ('serpent'): Juliet is, for a moment, appalled that her fair lover could have done such a thing, and throughout this speech compares his apparently deceptive mildness with the deceptive appearance of the 'fiend' Satan; but when the Nurse agrees that men are all deceivers, Juliet recovers her faith in Romeo very quickly indeed
bower:	enclose, embower
naught:	wicked
dissemblers:	deceivers
aqua vitae:	reviving alcoholic drink
fain:	willingly, gladly
needly . . . ranked:	must be accompanied
modern:	ordinary
sound:	express
wot:	know

Act III Scene 3

Time: late on Monday evening (III.3.164, 172)

In the previous scene we saw how Juliet reacted to the news of Tybalt's death and Romeo's banishment; we now see how Romeo responds to his bad fortune. Since killing Tybalt he has hidden in Friar Laurence's cell (III.2.141). The Friar now tells him that he is banished by the Prince which, as it means separation from Juliet, is to Romeo only another way of condemning him to death. The Nurse comes, as she had promised Juliet she would (III.2.140–1), and her description of Juliet's grief so fills Romeo with guilt and regret that he tries to kill himself. Horrified at this, the Friar in a long speech shows Romeo the folly of suicide; tells him that he has much to be thankful for; urges him to go that night to Juliet, as arranged (II.4.183–7; II.5.72–4), to comfort her; and then to leave Verona for Mantua, where he may live until such time as the Friar can publicly proclaim the marriage, reconcile the families and gain a pardon from the Prince. To all this, Romeo agrees. The Nurse leaves to tell Juliet that Romeo is coming, and the scene ends with the Friar warning Romeo to leave Verona with care, and assuring him that he will keep in touch with him through Romeo's servant (Balthasar).

NOTES AND GLOSSARY:

fearful:	frightened, full of fear
parts:	personal qualities
vanished from:	escaped from (and so vanished into air)
without:	outside, beyond
deadly sin:	the Friar exclaims at what seems to him to be the sin of ingratitude for what is, legally, mercy, since the Prince could have had Romeo put to death
rushed:	this is a strange word, perhaps a printer's error for 'brushed' or 'thrust'
validity:	value
Still blush:	Romeo thinks Juliet's lips will blush for 'kissing' each other when they touch
mean:	means
though . . . mean:	however distasteful
mangle:	mutilate, torture
fond:	foolish
Yet:	still
displant:	move
prevails not:	cannot prevail in argument, convince
dispute:	discuss

thy estate:	your position, the state of your affairs
simpleness:	folly; Romeo's folly is that he remains lying on the ground and will not hide
woeful sympathy:	Romeo 'sympathises', or identifies, with Juliet in that he behaves exactly like her in his grief (or 'woe')
O:	the sound of moaning
level:	aim
sack:	plunder
Unseemly:	improper, unbecoming
ill-beseeming:	inappropriate, unnatural
tempered:	moderated, balanced
wit:	intellectual ability
Which:	you who
bedeck:	decorate
but:	only
Digressing:	if it deviates
Killing:	if it kills
flask:	container for gunpowder
dead:	wishing to be dead
There:	in that respect
mishaved:	misbehaved
Watch is set:	at nightfall the city gates would be closed and a guard ('Watch') set
blaze:	proclaim
comfort:	cheerfulness
Sojourn:	live
hap:	happening
chances:	occurs
brief:	with so brief a farewell, that is, hurriedly

Act III Scene 4

Time: night-time, very early Tuesday morning (III.4.5–7, 34–5)

We have not seen the lovers together since the short scene of their marriage (II.6). Since then, in III.2 and III.3, we have seen their separate reactions to the ill-fortune which has intervened, and we are now anxious to see them together to take their farewell (in what will prove to be their last scene together until their deaths). However, Shakespeare keeps the audience in anticipation by turning aside for a moment to introduce a new complication, a new stroke of fate which is to hasten the tragedy. He had prepared for this in I.2–3 when we learned of Paris's suit for Juliet. Then Capulet had said that he would follow Juliet's wishes in the matter (I.2.16–19), but, now that Tybalt's death has so disturbed the family as to prevent his discussing it with her, he tells Paris that he is sure Juliet will obey him as her father and so he goes ahead to arrange the marriage for Thursday without consulting Juliet. His wife, Lady Capulet, is to tell her (*not* ask her). If we recollect how obedient Juliet was in I.3 we can understand why Capulet should be so sure that she will obey him now. He is, of course, proved wrong, and the scene underlines this in an ironic way. There is a contrast implied between this marriage arranged by parents and the marriage, resulting from love, which is about to be consummated in Juliet's room. Juliet has now moved far from I.3; her parents act as though she is still the same girl, but she is now, unknown to them, married and awaiting her bridegroom.

NOTES AND GLOSSARY:

fallen out:	worked out
unluckily:	unfortunately
move:	persuade
promise:	assure
but . . . company:	if you had not been here
mewed . . . heaviness:	shut up with her grief; Juliet's real cause of grief is, of course, not Tybalt's death, as her mother supposes, but Romeo's banishment, and she is shut up in her room only for Romeo to come to her
desperate tender:	bold offer
keep . . . ado:	not have an elaborate ceremony with many guests
late:	recently
held . . . carelessly:	did not esteem ('held') him dearly
'A:	on
ere you go to bed:	this introduces a moment's suspence: it was late at night that Romeo left the Friar (III.3.172), and if Lady Capulet goes now to Juliet's room she will either find Romeo there or be there when he arrives; Lady Capulet does, in fact, disturb the lovers (III.5.39–40)
against:	for

Act III Scene 5

Time: dawn on Tuesday (III.5.1–2, 6–10, 40)

We do not see Romeo arrive at Juliet's room, but we do witness the parting of the lovers. It is now nearly dawn, so some time has passed since Romeo left the Friar late on Monday night (III.3.172), and we are to suppose that during the night Romeo has been with Juliet and consummated their marriage. Indeed, it adds to the irony of III.4 if Romeo is actually with Juliet as her father is arranging her marriage to Paris. This would mean that the secret love match is being consummated (and so confirmed emotionally and legally) even as Capulet plans a public wedding for Juliet.

In this, only the fourth scene in which they have been together (I.5, II.2, II.6), the lovers have to admit that day is dawning and they must part or Romeo will be captured and put to death for not going into exile (as the Prince had decreed, III.1.194–5). The Nurse interrupts them to say that Juliet's mother is coming (as she had been told to do by Capulet, III.4.15, 31), and so Romeo leaves. Juliet, filled with misgivings, fears that they will never meet again. Although we cannot yet be sure she is right, Juliet's fears increase *our* fear that the tragedy is now gathering momentum.

Just as Juliet has bid her husband farewell, she is told by her mother that in two days she must marry Paris. Lady Capulet says that Juliet's father has arranged this so as to stop her grieving for Tybalt. He wants her to have an occasion for joy. Paris himself gives the same explanation in the next scene (IV.1.9–15), and this would explain why Capulet went ahead in III.4 without consulting Juliet. It is another example of tragic irony: hoping to make Juliet happy Capulet in fact achieves the exact opposite and contributes to those circumstances which bring about her death.

Juliet flatly refuses the marriage and, when her father comes in, he is furious at this disobedience, shocking both the Nurse and Lady Capulet by the violence of his anger and the insults he hurls at Juliet. He swears that unless Juliet obeys him he will never see her again. In comic contrast, the Nurse happily suggests that Juliet should indeed marry Paris as Romeo is unlikely ever to be able to return. Juliet is naturally appalled at this, and, as Romeo had sought out the Friar when he wished to marry Juliet (II.3) and after killing Tybalt (III.3), so, in this new difficulty, Juliet decides to go to him for help.

NOTES AND GLOSSARY:

fearful:	frightened
yond:	yonder
envious:	malicious
jocund:	merry
and live:	if I am to stay alive
exhales:	draws up; meteors were thought to be drawn up from the earth and set on fire by the sun
so:	if
reflex:	reflection

Cynthia:	goddess of the moon
Nor that is not:	nor is that
care:	desire, concern
sharps:	musical notes
division:	music; Juliet puns on the word in the next line
Some . . . eyes:	the toad, having more beautiful eyes than the lark, was said to have exchanged his eyes for the lark's, as the lark is the more beautiful creature
hunt's up:	early morning song to wake huntsmen; as newly married couples were similarly awakened, the term was used in this context too
be . . . years:	have aged many years
an . . . soul:	a soul which foresees bad fortune
trust:	believe
procures:	brings
how now:	how are you
still:	always
feeling:	deeply felt: Juliet's mother believes Juliet means the death of Tybalt; we know it is the loss of Romeo she feels deeply
friend:	to her mother this means Tybalt; to us, Romeo
asunder:	apart
venge:	avenge
runagate:	renegade
dram:	small drink; Lady Capulet means poison; ironically, it will be Romeo who poisons himself
That . . . company:	that is, he too will die
dead:	Juliet is deliberately ambiguous: to her mother she says she wants Romeo dead; her true meaning is that her heart is dead as Romeo has left
temper:	her mother takes Juliet to mean 'mix'; we take the meaning 'moderate' or 'weaken'
wreak:	avenge
careful:	considerate
sorted out:	arranged
sudden:	unexpected
in happy time:	opportunely (ironically said)
he . . . be:	he that wants to be my
at your hands:	from you
brother's:	brother-in-law's (see III.1.146)
conduit:	water pipe (Juliet is crying)
bark:	boat
overset:	overturn
will none:	will have none of it

Take me with you: let me understand you
proud: grateful, pleased
wrought: arranged
bride: bridegroom
proud: pleased
But . . . love: but I am grateful that you have arranged something for me, even though I hate it when you intended me to love it
chopped logic: hair splitting, quibbling with words
minion: worthless girl
fettle: groom a horse, that is, get ready, prepare
joints: limbs, that is, her body, herself
hurdle: sledge
green . . . carrion: pallid as a corpse
baggage: hussy, good-for-nothing
tallow: hard, yellowy fat from which candles were made
Hang thee: may you be hanged
fingers itch: that is, itch to strike her
lent: given; in Christian thought all things on earth are but lent to us during our lives
hilding: worthless girl
rate: berate, scold
Prudence: probably not the Nurse's real Christian name, but used sarcastically by Capulet
Smatter . . . gossips: chatter with your friends, and not with me
God . . . e'en: in bidding her good evening Capulet is telling the Nurse to go
gravity: wisdom (Capulet is being ironic)
God's bread: the bread blessed in the Holy Communion service
matched: married
demesnes: estates, lands
puling: whining, whimpering
mammet: puppet
in . . . tender: when fortune makes her an offer
an: if
Graze: feed: Capulet insults Juliet by using a word applied to animals
house: live in my house
do not use: am not accustomed
Advise: consider
Nor . . . good: nor shall anything of mine ever help you
forsworn: break my word
a word: that is, a word to your father on your behalf
faith: vow, that is, her marriage vow

practise stratagems: use cunning schemes
all . . . nothing: it is a safe bet
challenge: claim
dishclout: dishcloth
Beshrew . . . heart: curse me if I'm wrong
Ancient damnation: damned old woman
compare: comparison
twain: two, that is, separated

Act IV Scene 1

Time: Tuesday (IV.1.90), *and, as both Paris and Juliet have come straight to the Friar following conversations near dawn on Tuesday, the morning of that day.*

In this scene Juliet and her suitor, Paris, meet for the only time in the play. Paris has come to see the Friar to tell him of his planned marriage with Juliet. He explains that the haste is because Capulet wants to lessen his daughter's grief at Tybalt's death. Juliet enters (she had resolved to visit the Friar at the end of III.5), and carefully avoids answering directly Paris's questions about her love for him and their marriage. Paris leaves, thinking Juliet is to confess to the Friar. In fact, she implores his help in avoiding the marriage with Paris. The Friar suggests that the night before her wedding (that is, tomorrow, Wednesday, night) she should take a potion he can give her which will make her appear to be dead but from the effects of which she will awake unharmed, as from a sleep. When she is found on her wedding day, all will think her dead, and she will be placed in the Capulet vault. The Friar, meanwhile, will inform Romeo of the plan by letter, and he and Romeo will be there when Juliet awakes. Romeo can then take her back to Mantua with him. To this desperate plan Juliet agrees.

NOTES AND GLOSSARY:
And . . . haste: no reluctance of mine will lessen his haste
Uneven: irregular, contrary to normal practice
counts: accounts, considers
sway: influence
minded . . . alone: remembered or dwelt upon when she is alone
price: value
abused: spoilt, marred
it: that is, her face
to my face: directly, and, about my face
not mine own: because, although Paris does not know this, it is Romeo's

entreat . . . alone:	ask you to leave us alone at this time
shield:	forbid
compass:	limit
prorogue:	delay, postpone
presently:	immediately
label:	seal, that is, confirm another marriage by holding another hand
deed:	legal document, that is, a binding marriage certificate
this:	this knife
extremes:	desperate situation
commission:	authority
Hold:	wait
shame:	disgrace, loss of honour
that:	you who
copest with:	encounters
it:	that is, shame
charnel house:	small building next to a church in which were placed bones disturbed when new graves were dug
reeky shanks:	damp and stinking shin-bones
chapless:	jawless
unstained:	faithful, not stained with infidelity
vial:	small bottle
distilling liquor:	drink which will spread through the body
humour:	liquid in the body which was thought to cause feeling
native progress:	natural movement
surcease:	stop
wanny:	wan, pale
supple government:	ability to move
against . . . awake:	in preparation for your awakening
drift:	purpose, plan
inconstant toy:	whim
prosperous:	successful

Act IV Scene 2

Time: 'near night' on Tuesday (IV.2.39)

Act IV Scene 1 could only have taken place on Tuesday morning as both Paris and Juliet visit the Friar directly after their conversation in III.4 and III.5 at dawn on Tuesday. In this scene Juliet returns straight from that visit to the Friar, so it cannot yet be, as Capulet says, 'late' on Tuesday. In the theatre we would not notice this: Shakespeare shortens the time-scale for dramatic effect so that we come quickly to the crucial Tuesday night.

In the Capulet house preparations are going forward for the wedding. Juliet, falling in with the Friar's plan, submits entirely to her father, who is so pleased that he brings forward the wedding to the next day, Wednesday. It is a cruel irony that Juliet's pretended change of heart is thus so effective that it contributes to the tragedy, for that lost day will help prevent Romeo learning the truth about the Friar's plan. Since the change of day will mean still less time for preparation, Capulet will himself stay up all night to help to get things ready in time. The scene ends on an ironic note: Capulet's heart is 'wondrous light' now that Juliet has agreed to marry Paris: the audience knows she has quite other intentions.

NOTES AND GLOSSARY:

cunning:	skilful
ill:	bad
try:	test
they . . . fingers:	proverbially the mark of a good cook
unfurnished:	unprepared in not having the necessary food ready
it:	she
harlotry:	waywardness
gadding:	wandering
behests:	commands
enjoined:	constrained, made
becomed:	proper
closet:	room
stir about:	busy myself

Act IV Scene 3

Time: Tuesday night (IV.3.12–3)

Juliet sends away the Nurse (as the Friar had directed, IV.1.92) and takes the potion. As the marriage is now on Wednesday, not Thursday, she is taking it a day earlier than the Friar had planned (IV.1.89–94). Juliet's soliloquy, dwelling on her fear of the vault, enlarges what she had already said to the Friar (IV.1.80–8) and darkens the atmosphere of death which is gathering in the play. By referring us yet again to the Capulet vault, the speech confirms us in our fear that in some way it is connected with the tragic climax of the play.

NOTES AND GLOSSARY:

attires:	clothes
orisons:	prayers

state:	condition
cross:	perverse
culled:	selected
behoveful:	needed
state:	ceremony
thrills:	shivers
ministered:	provided
tried:	proved
strangled:	suffocated
like:	likely
conceit:	imagining
receptacle:	sepulchre
festering:	rotting
mandrake:	a plant which was said to shriek when pulled out of the ground and so drive mad anyone who uprooted it
distraught:	mad
environed:	surrounded
rage:	madness
spit:	pierce through, impale

Act IV Scene 4

Time: 3 a.m. on Wednesday (IV.4.3–4)

This is a dramatically effective short interlude such as Shakespeare often devised in order to give the audience a moment's relief and to highlight crucial scenes by contrast. Capulet has been up all night helping to prepare the wedding feast. This scene gives us a glimpse of the excitement and fun of these preparations, with Capulet good-naturedly joking with the servants and ordering them about, hurrying everyone as much as he can. It is a scene of happy and boisterous confusion, in studied contrast to the sombre quiet of Juliet's soliloquy in IV.3 and the outbursts of grief which are to follow in IV.5.

Furthermore, we are aware that, apart from this noisy preparation and excited anticipation of the wedding, alone in her room, Juliet has taken the potion which will bring all this furious activity to nothing. In much the same way, Capulet's plans to marry Juliet to Paris in III.4 had been rendered ironic by our knowledge that, even as he spoke, Juliet was either with, or waiting for, Romeo in her room. In each case the audience has a fuller knowledge of the situation than have the characters on the stage and, because of this, the audience knows that what the characters are doing will come to nothing. In III.4 we knew, and Capulet did not, that Juliet was already married; here, we know, and Capulet does not, that Juliet will go to the vault as if dead and not to her wedding with Paris. Such an ironic mood is characteristic of tragedy; the audience can see that the plans being made by characters in the play will not turn out as they expect.

Finally, the scene gives the impression of time passing: it fills in the night while Juliet is drugged, for, at the end of the scene, we are told that the bridegroom, Paris, has arrived. Thus, it bridges Tuesday night (IV.3) and Wednesday morning (IV.5).

NOTES AND GLOSSARY:

pastry:	part of the kitchen
curfew bell:	bell that tolls the hour
baked meats:	meat pies
cot-quean:	man who does woman's work (as Capulet had promised he would, IV.2.43)
watching:	staying awake
whit:	bit
mouse hunt:	up at night after a woman
watch . . . now:	watch you to make sure you don't go off at night like that now
jealous-hood:	jealous woman
have . . . that will:	have brains enough to
Mass:	a common exclamation, from 'By the Mass'
whoreson:	rascally fellow
loggerhead:	blockhead, a pun on 'logs' in lines 16 and 18
Good Father:	an exclamation, perhaps a misprint for the common 'Good Faith'
trim:	dress

Act IV Scene 5

Time: early Wednesday morning, straight after IV.5 (IV.4.25–8; IV.5.1)

The Nurse goes to wake Juliet and finds her apparently dead. We should notice that, for the first time in the play, the Nurse is not in Juliet's confidence, and is deceived like everyone else. The Friar arrives and, amidst the exclamations of grief, takes charge to ensure that Juliet is carried to the family vault as he had planned.

Shakespeare carefully prevents the audience's sympathies from being too deeply aroused in this scene, for the real cause of grief is yet to come with the true death of Juliet. The exaggerated language of the laments of the Nurse, Paris and Capulet, which almost become ridiculous; the Friar's speeches, which remind the audience that this is all part of a plan; and the comedy of the musicians with which the scene ends, all tend to stop us becoming too involved in the sorrow of the household.

NOTES AND GLOSSARY:

Fast:	fast asleep
pennyworths:	allowances of sleep
set up his rest:	to stake all one's money at the card game of primero, and so the meaning here is 'is determined'; the Nurse means that Paris will keep Juliet awake the next night by making love to her
settled:	congealed
deflowered by him:	lost her virginity to him
lasting:	endless, everlasting
solace in:	take comfort in
catched:	snatched
Beguiled:	deceived
spited:	treated spitefully
Uncomfortable:	depriving us of our comfort
solemnity:	ceremony
confusion:	calamity, disaster
confusions:	disorders
Your part:	that is, her body
his part:	that is, her soul
rosemary:	a herb, symbolising remembrance
Yet . . . merriment:	reason, which knows there is no real cause for grief, laughs at the tears which natural affection makes us shed
lour:	frown
put . . . pipes:	pack up our things
case:	situation
case:	container for a musical instrument
Heart's ease:	a popular song of the time
'My . . . full':	another song
give . . . soundly:	play it loudly and pay you back for refusing
gleek:	mockery, scorn
give . . . minstrel:	call you a good-for-nothing
serving-creature:	like 'minstrel' a term of derision; 'serving creature' is even more insulting than 'serving-man'
pate:	head
carry no crotchets:	tolerate none of your whims; literally, 'crotchets' are musical notes
re . . . fa:	musical notes
note:	understand or pay attention, a pun on 'note' meaning 'set to music'

put out:	display
When . . . sound:	the beginning of a published poem in praise of music
griping:	agonising
dumps:	depression
Catling:	a lute string, and so a humorous surname for a musician
Rebeck:	a fiddle
Soundpost:	part of a violin
cry you mercy:	beg you pardon
for sounding:	for making music

Act V Scene 1

Time: later on Wednesday

It is not clear from the scene itself on which day it occurs. We do know that the last scene of the play is set during the night that follows the day of this scene. Romeo is here in Mantua, and says that he will be back in Verona to lie with Juliet 'tonight' (V.1.26, 34), and in V.3 we see him arrive at the vault. But is this scene set on Wednesday, the day of Juliet's entombment (IV.5), or on Thursday? In other words, does Romeo kill himself on the night following Juliet's supposed 'death' or twenty-four hours later?

On the one hand, the Friar had said that Juliet would be drugged for forty-two hours (IV.1.105). As she took the potion on Tuesday night (IV.3), she would wake up on Thursday night. For Romeo to be there when she wakes in V.3 his 'tonight' should mean Thursday night, which would place this scene on Thursday. Later in the play, just after Juliet has woken, the Watch says she has been in the vault for two days (V.3.176), so V.3, set when it is dark, just before dawn, seems to occur very early on Friday (so that Juliet has been in the tomb on Wednesday and Thursday, two days). This again points to this scene being set on Thursday.

On the other hand, however, we learn that Balthasar left Verona immediately after seeing Juliet laid in the vault on Wednesday morning (V.1.20–1) and as Romeo intends to be back in Verona 'tonight' the journey between Mantua and Verona does not take long. Hence, Balthasar could arrive in Mantua on Wednesday, the day he seems to have left Verona. Another piece of evidence also suggests Wednesday for this scene. V.3 begins with Paris performing funeral rites at Juliet's tomb, rites he says he will perform every night hereafter (V.3.16–17). It would be natural, therefore, to suppose this is the first time he has done this, which would mean this is the first night

Juliet has been in the vault, namely Wednesday. He would hardly promise to perform these rites every night on the *second* night he visited her tomb. And this, again, would point to our scene here as on Wednesday, since Romeo meets Paris at the Capulet vault.

In the theatre, no one is likely to remember the Friar's forty-two hours, or notice the Watch's reference to two days. The sequence of events is clear, and the impression is of a *short* passage of time. Watching the play, it would seem that this scene follows immediately after IV.5, that is, that it is still Wednesday. Balthasar's comment on the haste with which he has come to Romeo (V.1.21) would reinforce this impression. Although, reading the play, we can notice evidence which suggests Thursday, no one in a theatre is going to be able to scrutinise the text in the way we have. And we must always remember that Shakespeare wrote not to be read, but to be watched. That is why he can be careless about details. The Friar's forty-two hours in fact fits neither Wednesday nor Thursday night exactly, counting from Tuesday night! Shakespeare almost certainly gave him that line for its *immediate* dramatic effect: it would make the Friar's plan sound like a carefully arranged scheme. Shakespeare knew it would slip from the audience's mind. Indeed, we should not call him 'careless' even: we only get into these difficulties if we read the plays like *novels,* but this is discussed further in the section on the plot of the play (p.78).

The Friar's plan of feigning Juliet's death, successfully carried out in IV.5, was intended to solve the lovers' problems. In this, the very next scene, we learn that Fate is not to be so easily thwarted. Romeo, who left Juliet early on Tuesday morning in II.5, is now in Mantua. As the scene opens, he is confidently expecting good news from Verona. These hopes are dashed immediately his servant, Balthasar, arrives to tell him Juliet is dead. Although the Friar had arranged to send news to Romeo in his exile through Balthasar (III.3.169–71), Balthasar has no letters from the Friar for Romeo and clearly does not know the truth about Juliet's 'death'. Romeo resolves to return to Verona that night, to poison himself at the vault where Juliet lies. He buys a poison for his purpose from an apothecary in Mantua.

NOTES AND GLOSSARY:

If . . . sleep:	if I may believe as true the dreams that come in sleep, even though they flatter my hopes by telling me what I wish to hear
presage:	portend, foretell
bosom's lord:	that is, his heart
how . . . joy:	when dreams of love are so full of joy, how sweet love must be in reality
presently:	immediately

took post:	post horses were swift horses available for hire at regular intervals on main roads, and so the phrase means 'to set out quickly by horse': by this means Romeo plans to return to Verona (lines 26 and 33)
office:	business
import:	suggest, signify
misadventure:	tragically ill-advised undertaking
Tush:	an exclamation of impatience
see for:	look for
apothecary:	druggist, a man who made and sold drugs and medicines
'a:	he
noted:	noticed
weeds:	drab clothes
Culling . . . simple:	picking plants from which to make medicines
account:	collection, number
bladders:	used to contain liquid
packthread:	strong thread or twine
old . . . roses:	rose petals pressed into small tablets
penury:	great poverty
Whose . . . death:	for the sale of which the penalty is immediate death
caitiff wretch:	miserable or wretched creature
there is:	that is, there in my hand
ducats:	gold coins, each worth nearly ten shillings in Elizabethan money, so Romeo is offering nearly £20, a very large sum then
soon-speeding gear:	quick-acting stuff
any he:	any man
utters:	sells
starveth . . . eyes:	appear in your starving face
dispatch:	send away your soul, that is, kill you
compounds:	mixtures
cordial:	restorative drink (as it will restore him to Juliet)

Act V Scene 2

Time: Wednesday

We learn from this short scene that the letter Friar Laurence had said he would send Romeo explaining the plan (IV.1.113–5) has not been delivered. Friar John, who was to have taken it, was shut up by health officers in a house in Verona which was thought to be plague-ridden. Friar Laurence must now go to the vault alone (he, of course, does not know that Romeo has also determined to go there). Following V.1 this scene confirms our fear that Romeo will not find out the truth about Juliet's 'death'. Quickly and simply things have gone terribly wrong since IV.5.

NOTES AND GLOSSARY:

barefoot brother: friar
associate: accompany; friars usually worked in pairs
searchers: men who searched out the plague by checking dead bodies, health officers
infectious pestilence: plague
reign: ruled, that is, the inhabitants of the house were infected
sealed up the doors: this was common practice with houses where people had the plague, to prevent it from spreading by stopping them from leaving their homes
brotherhood: religious order
nice: trivial
charge: serious matter
dear import: great importance
danger: damage, harm
crow: crow-bar
beshrew: blame
accidents: doings, events, that is, Juliet's proposed marriage to Paris and the Friar's plan to prevent it

---

Act V Scene 3

Time: Wednesday night to near dawn on Thursday (V.3.188–9, 305–6)

The tragic catastrophe is presented in the play's final, and longest, scene. The play had opened with a scene which brought to the stage the Capulets, Montagues and the Prince; its turning point in III.1 had again assembled these characters, and now, at the end, all are brought together once more. But whereas in I.1 and III.1 it was the continuance of their feud which had brought them together, now it is the ending of that feud and their reconciliation through the tragic deaths of their heirs, deaths for which, as the Prince himself says as the scene draws to a close, they and their hatred were responsible.

The scene which thus concludes the action is remarkable for its variety. It begins with Paris coming to grieve at Juliet's tomb. His funeral rites establish a suitably sombre mood. But Paris is disturbed by Romeo, who has arrived from Mantua to poison himself at the vault. As Romeo begins to open the tomb, Paris steps forward to stop him. Paris believes that grief for Tybalt's death, which Romeo caused, killed Juliet, and that Romeo, as a Montague, has now come to mutilate the dead bodies of the Capulets Tybalt and Juliet. Appalled by this, he attempts to arrest Romeo. In the ensuing fight, Paris is killed. Ironically, this is the first time Juliet's two lovers have met on stage, and it is only after killing him that Romeo recognises Paris.

After this sudden violence, the mood changes again as Romeo opens the vault and, in a long soliloquy, meditates on Juliet's beauty and prepares himself for death. Just as he has drunk the poison, the Friar arrives, and, finding the bodies of Paris and Romeo, he tells the waking Juliet to fly from the place. When she realises Romeo is dead, Juliet refuses to leave and stabs herself. The Watch has been summoned by Paris's servant, and there is considerable confusion as the Capulets, Montagues and the Prince are summoned and all wonder at how these three deaths can have occurred. The Friar explains what has happened, and the scene ends in quiet sadness as Capulet and Montague are reconciled.

NOTES AND GLOSSARY:

Hence . . . aloof:	go from here and keep away
all along:	at full length
loose:	that is, the earth is loose
As:	as a
stand:	wait
adventure:	dare
Sweet flower:	that is, Juliet
strew:	cover by scattering
canopy:	covering
sweet:	perfumed
wanting:	lacking
obsequies:	funeral rites
cross:	interfere with
Muffle:	hide, conceal
mattock:	tool like a pickaxe
letter:	this Romeo had written before leaving Mantua (V.1.25)
charge:	command
course:	business
jealous:	inquisitive, suspicious
hungry:	because Death is never satisfied
intents:	intentions
empty:	and therefore hungry and savage
For . . . same:	all the same

I fear:	give me reason to be afraid of what he will do
maw:	stomach
womb:	belly
in despite:	to spite you (by forcing more 'food' in when the 'maw' is already 'gorged')
apprehend:	arrest
unhallowed:	evil
thou must die:	the punishment for returning from banishment
these gone:	these buried in the vault
For . . . myself:	for I come here armed as my own enemy (because he has the poison to kill himself)
conjuration:	literally, casting of a magic spell; Paris means that he defies Romeo's attempt to put him off by solemn words
Watch:	police
betossed:	tossed hither and thither (by Fortune)
triumphant:	glorious
lantern:	windowed upper part of a building which admits light, but Romeo, rather than promising Paris a particular kind of tomb, is saying, metaphorically, that this vault is a lantern because it is lit by Juliet's beauty (lines 85–6)
feasting presence:	festival presence chamber, that is, the room in which a monarch would receive guests and visitors
keepers:	jailers
A . . . death:	a proverbial phrase, describing a sudden burst of vigour just before death
ensign:	flag, banner
sheet:	winding sheet in which corpses are wrapped
To . . . enemy:	to separate from his youth him who was your enemy, that is, kill myself
paramour:	lover
And . . . flesh:	free this body, tired of the world, from the influence of hostile stars
dateless:	endless, eternal
conduct:	conductor, that is, the poison, which Romeo here addresses
desperate pilot:	that is, himself
true Apothecary:	the Apothecary spoke the truth (in V.1.77–9)
stumbled:	there was an old superstition that to stumble is a sign that what one is doing will not turn out well
at:	over, on
Bliss:	the eternal bliss of salvation in heaven
vainly:	in vain

unthrifty:	unlucky
dreamt:	Balthasar would actually have seen this happen: perhaps he does not want to believe that what he saw is true; perhaps (remembering it is night in a graveyard) he really does think it was a dream or hallucination; or again, perhaps he is afraid to say openly that such an awful thing has happened
masterless:	abandoned (by their masters or owners)
gory:	bloody
discoloured:	stained (with blood)
steeped:	soaked
unkind:	unnatural
comfortable:	comforting
contagion:	contagious disease, foul influence
cup:	Romeo had evidently poured the poison into a cup to drink it (the apothecary had said that the poison should be taken as a drink, V.1.77–8)
timeless:	both 'untimely' and 'endless'
churl:	a mean person, here used as an affectionate rebuke
restorative:	that is, her kiss
attach:	arrest
ground:	cause, explanation
without:	without knowing the
startles . . . ears:	shocks you
comes:	comes about
instruments:	tools
house:	that is, sheath
warns:	tolls, summons
conspires:	plots
untaught:	ill-mannered, used here affectionately and in sad jest
press before:	hurry ahead of; it was, of course, bad manners to enter a room in front of a parent
mouth . . . outrage:	passionate outcry, cries of grief
spring:	source of a stream, and so, cause; the metaphor is carried on in 'head', the beginning of a stream, and 'descent'
general:	leader
And . . . patience:	and let patience rule us in our response to misfortune
greatest:	that is, the one most suspect
direful:	dreadful, awful
both . . . excused:	both to accuse myself and to defend myself; the Friar means that he knows he is guilty in that his

	scheme caused these deaths, and yet he is innocent for that was never his intention
in:	about
date of breath:	span or time of breath, that is, life
stolen:	secret
You:	the Friar addresses the Capulets
Betrothed:	pledged to marry
perforce:	by force
mean:	means
form:	appearance
as:	on
closely:	secretly
privy:	accessory, in the secret
his:	its
We . . . man:	despite what you have just said, we have always known you are a holy man
post:	great haste
made your master:	was your master doing
make good:	confirm
therewithal:	with that
joys:	children
brace of kinsmen:	Mercutio and Paris were both related to the Prince
jointure:	marriage settlement given by the groom's family to the bride (the opposite of a dowry): Capulet means that Montague's handshake is all he can ask for as a settlement for Juliet
rate:	high value
Romeo's:	that is, Romeo's statue
lie:	Montague is thinking of the figures carved lying on tombs
glooming:	dark, meaning metaphorically 'sad'

Part 3

Commentary

Plot and structure: realism and romance

Simple structure

Romeo and Juliet is firmly centred on the figures of its hero and heroine. Although characters like the Nurse and Mercutio are fully developed and have large parts, it is the story of Romeo and Juliet that holds our attention. There is no sub-plot, no secondary story, such as Shakespeare and other Elizabethan dramatists often introduced into their plays. We are never long away from either Romeo or Juliet, and the course of their love is hence clearly before us throughout the play. In Act I Romeo and Juliet meet and fall in love; in Act II they declare their love and are secretly married; they try to overcome the obstacles to their love which arise in Act III by the schemes of Acts III and IV, but these efforts are tragically frustrated in Act V. We thus have a clear structure: an optimistic and often comic movement up to the marriage at the end of Act II is followed by a counter-movement, which begins with the quarrel in III.1 and leads to tragedy. This clear design means that there is something relentless about the progress of the play. Shakespeare does, as we shall see in a moment, vary mood and pace a good deal, but there is no extended digression or relief from the tragic tale.

Time in the play

This is emphasised by the time-scale of the play. We saw that the compression of events into a few days was one of Shakespeare's most significant changes to the story as it occurred in his source (p.19). The action of the play lasts only four days. From Capulet's question 'What day is this?', to which Paris replies 'Monday, my lord' (III.4.18–19), we can work out on which day each scene occurs. In the theatre, of course, we could not do this. What matters as we watch the play is not the actual day but the short sequence of time. That Romeo and Juliet marry only the day after they first met (that is, very soon after!) is the point, not that they meet on a Sunday and marry on a Monday. Nevertheless, it is easier to distinguish the days by their names in discussion than in any other way, and doing this we may summarise the sequence of events as follows.

Act I opens at 9 a.m. on Sunday morning (I.1.161) and culminates in Capulet's party on Sunday evening. Act II takes us through Sunday night to dawn on Monday (II.2.176; II.3.1–2) and to the marriage of the lovers in II.6 on Monday afternoon (II.4.176–9). The quarrel that opens Act III is later on Monday afternoon (III.1.112–13), and by III.4.34–5 it is late that night. Romeo leaves Juliet in III.5 as the dawn breaks on Tuesday, and Juliet's marriage to Paris, originally planned for Thursday (III.4.17–21) is brought forward to the next day, Wednesday (IV.2.23–37). Early on Wednesday morning Juliet is discovered apparently dead (IV.5.3–4). Later that day Romeo learns, as he thinks, of Juliet's death, and that night kills himself at her tomb. The play ends as dawn is about to break on Thursday (V.3.188–9, 305–6). The play thus lasts from Sunday morning until the night of the following Wednesday/Thursday.

Such a short and consistent (even allowing for the slight difficulty about V.1 discussed on pp.65–6) time-scale is very rare in Elizabethan drama. By keeping the sequence of events clearly before the audience Shakespeare makes the tragedy the more pitiful simply because of the swiftness with which events occur. The action seems to rush on at headlong speed. 'I stand on sudden haste' says Romeo (II.3.89), and he does seem to be engaged in a race against time. Everything in the play happens at great speed; it is as though it *has* to happen so. The lovers hurry into marriage, and Romeo is immediately hurried into banishment. The moment Romeo hears of Juliet's death he posts back to Verona to kill himself. In all this haste, the love of Romeo and Juliet is very short-lived. Of Romeo's avowal of love Juliet says:

> Although I joy in thee,
> I have no joy of this contract tonight.
> It is too rash, too unadvised, too sudden;
> Too like the lightning, which doth cease to be
> Ere one can say 'It lightens'.

> (II.2.116–20)

Lightning is but momentary. As Romeo prepares to kill himself he uses the word again:

> How oft when men are at the point of death
> Have they been merry! which their keepers call
> A lightning before death. O how may I
> Call this a lightning?

> (V.3.88–91)

Because of the time-scale of the play the love of Romeo and Juliet does

seem to be a 'lightning before death'. It has no sooner come to them
than it is taken from them.

Coincidences and improbabilities in the action

The main line of the action may be clear and the structure of the play
simple, but to set down the story in bald prose may well make it sound
incredible. Even if we allow that two young people could fall so
completely in love so suddenly as do Romeo and Juliet, can we also
allow that they would change so completely to do so? Romeo, we
know, is infatuated with Rosaline to an extraordinary degree. His
melancholy behaviour because she rejects him is the first thing we
learn about him (I.1.116–238) and his anguished passion is the butt of
Mercutio's jokes in I.4 and II.1. For her part, Juliet, when we first meet
her, has no thoughts of love or marriage, and is fully prepared to follow
her parents' wishes in looking favourably on Paris (I.3.67, 98–100).
And yet, in a moment, Romeo forgets Rosaline (I.5.44–53) and Juliet
is thinking of marriage to an enemy (I.5.134–5). Even if we think we
can accept that two young people would change so completely, can we
really believe that any friar would concoct such an elaborate plan as
Friar Laurence does, involving a potion which is almost magical in its
effect?

On top of these central elements in the plot there is an extraordinary amount of coincidence in the play. A few coincidences could
happen to anyone, but can we believe that as many as are in this play
(and *all* unfortunate, at that) could happen in so few days? That
Romeo should fall in love with the daughter of an enemy house is, of
course, the central, tragic, chance event. That Paris should come as
suitor to Juliet at just this time is another coincidence which hastens
the tragedy. That Friar Laurence's letter should not be delivered is
another; that Romeo should kill himself *just before* Juliet awakes is
another; that the Friar should arrive at the vault *just after* Romeo has
taken poison, another. Had any of these chances fallen out differently
there would have been no tragedy. Romeo, for example, would have
found Juliet awake had he come a little later or she woken a little
earlier. Thinking of cases like this, it is hard not to feel that Romeo
and Juliet are killed by cruel chance, or Fate. If Romeo's luck had been
different, the Friar would have come sooner and told him the truth
about Juliet's 'death'. But Romeo has no luck in this play: he, and
Juliet, are the victims of an extraordinary succession (even an
incredible succession) of mischances. (This is discussed further on
pp.87–9.)

There are other odd things about the action of the play. When Juliet
is discovered apparently dead in IV.5, why does no one wonder why

she died? No one suspects suicide or foul play, and no one notices either the vial or the knife that must lie beside her (IV.3.20, 23). Why is it that the Friar, who expected Juliet to awake after forty-two hours (IV.1.104–5), arrives late at the vault on a matter of such urgency? How can Romeo, who has only just arrived in Mantua, have already discovered, and remembered, an apothecary's shop where he can buy poison? He had no idea he would ever need it, after all, and yet in V.1 it is immediately in his mind. Or again, why are Montagues and Capulets at each other's throats? What is the cause of their quarrel? We are never told. One last example: if we are to believe this feud stands in the way of Romeo's love for Juliet, what do we make of the fact that it did not stand in the way of his love for Rosaline? Rosaline was also a Capulet (I.2.68, 81–2), and yet Romeo had been able to see her because we know she refused him. If he could see her, why not Juliet?

Realism in the play

Clearly, we are not dealing with a *realistic* play. We should not be afraid to recognise and admit this. Realism is a comparatively recent literary convention. Living in the twentieth century, accustomed to reading novels, we tend to suppose that literature has always tried to represent everyday life as it really is. This is not the case. Indeed, it is only by recognising that Shakespeare's plays are *not* realistic that we can understand how they work. If we come to them expecting the kind of credible and coherent story we find in a novel, we shall be perplexed by the sort of unlikely coincidences, improbable events and inconsistencies that we have just noticed in *Romeo and Juliet*. We should have to conclude that the plays are incredible, even absurd.

The truth is that Shakespeare was not trying to construct that kind of story. He is casual about details and disregards realism because these things did not matter to him. That is why, although the play is set in Italy, there is no real attempt to present Italian customs accurately. Nowadays we expect authenticity in such things: in Shakespeare's play, however, Capulet's household is a typical English Elizabethan household; the masked dance at Capulet's party was fashionable in Elizabethan England and the description of the apothecary's shop (V.1.40–8) would have fitted many such shops in Elizabethan London; all through the play, proverbs, idioms and exclamations are thoroughly English. Indeed, at one point Mercutio makes fun of the Italian style of duelling which had recently become fashionable in England (II.4.19–26). This we would expect of an Englishman and it would go down well with an English audience: but Mercutio is supposed to be Italian!

The pattern of the action

Shakespeare's plays, then, are not made up of a coherent story, correct and accurate in all its details, believable in all its incidents. They are made of contrasts, comparisons, effective scenes and dramatic moments, such as we noticed in the scene summaries. It is because of this that a Shakespeare play is full of variety and incident. We should always remember that Shakespeare was a professional dramatist who had, above all, to draw audiences. We may think of *Romeo and Juliet* as a tragedy of love, but it is, in performance, a play of remarkably varied moods and actions, all carefully contrived by Shakespeare. The very first scene can show us how the whole play works. We begin with comedy from the servants, but even as we are laughing at them the mood changes, and before we know it there is a fight and a riot with citizens pouring on to the stage shouting and fighting. This uproar is suddenly silenced by the appearance of the Prince who, in another change of mood, delivers an impressive and threatening long speech to his subjects. The stage then clears and we listen now to new matter in a different tone. It is a family discussion about the peculiar behaviour of Romeo. This whets our appetite: we know Romeo is to be the hero of the play. When he comes on the scene ends as it had begun, with only two people talking, but now it is not the bawdy talk of the servants we hear but the sophisticated language of love. So, in only just over 200 lines, Shakespeare has given us merriment, spectacle and uneasiness; and he has also, of course, set the scene for the play. In just this way the audience's interest is maintained throughout the play. The quiet scene, II.6, is followed by the violence of III.1; Juliet's soliloquy in IV.3 contrasts with the bustle of IV.4; the comedy of the musicians which ends IV.5 contrasts with the outcries of grief earlier in that scene. Examples could be multiplied.

By such arrangements of the action Shakespeare makes watching one of his plays a varied and constantly surprising experience: we are never quite sure what to expect next. Of course, there is a story running through the whole play, and in a general way it holds together. But the kind of questions we were asking a moment ago about *Romeo and Juliet* cannot be answered because Shakespeare gives no answers. He was thinking in a different way. He likes to bring his characters together in what he knows will be a good scene: how he gets them there does not interest him nearly so much as the scene itself. The very characters themselves (as we shall see later, pp.98–100) are chosen not as 'real' human beings, but to contrast and complement each other in effective ways. So, to appreciate a play like *Romeo and Juliet* we need to forget our modern tastes and surrender ourselves to a romantic tale of love which does not belong to our ordinary everyday world of cause and effect.

This is not to say that the play is merely romance in the sense of a fanciful piece of art irrelevant to our lives. Far from it! Shakespeare neglects realistic detail in order to explore, poetically, themes and situations which may be called 'realistic' in a deeper sense. Another way of putting it would be to say that to Shakespeare the plot is only the starting-point. He uses it in order to gain effects, and these effects are what count. We could almost say that the story as such is the least important part of the play. It is Shakespeare's insight into his characters and their feelings that matters. Above all, it is the way his poetry expresses these feelings which affects us. Because of his poetry and his insight, we do not doubt the truth of the love that is shown in the play, however we may quibble about the *story* of the lovers. When Romeo and Juliet speak to each other in II.2 we hear a genuine love expressed. It is for that expression of genuine love that the plot exists. How Shakespeare manages so to capture ideas and emotions we must now consider.

Themes: love and hate

Romeo and Juliet is a play about love. With that statement we may all agree. Indeed, it may appear to be so obvious as not to be worth saying. And yet, if we explore into the play a little, we find it is 'about love' in a richer sense than we might at first suppose.

The change love causes in Romeo and Juliet

We meet in the play two young people who fall helplessly and completely in love with each other. When we first meet him, Romeo is a rather tiresome young man, endlessly complaining, in the elaborate language of love then fashionable, about his sorrows because Rosaline rejects him. He is playing the part of the Petrarchan lover. The love poetry of the medieval Italian poet Francesco Petrarch (1304–74) was widely imitated throughout the Renaissance. It established literary conventions of how to behave and how to talk when in love. In Elizabethan love poetry we meet, over and over again, lovers who behave just like Romeo. They dote upon one lady; live only for her; express their feelings in elaborate conceits (or extended images) and rhetorical phrases; they are devastated if she frowns on them and overwhelmed by joy if she smiles. It is an elaborate, exaggerated ideal, almost a religion of love.

Mercutio recognises the fashionable posturing of Romeo's behaviour when he says 'Now is he for the numbers that Petrarch flowed in'

(II.4.38–9). So Romeo regards Rosaline as beyond all women in beauty:

The all-seeing sun
Ne'er saw her match since first the world begun.

(I.2.91–2)

And he swears his love for her in religious terms – he worships her, and resorts to ingenious imagery to say so (for example I.2.87–90). He talks of his depression at her rejection of him in the same exaggerated way. It is difficult for us not to feel that he is wallowing in self-pity (for example I.1.186–94), and the oxymorons (combinations of words of opposite meanings) with which he endeavours to describe his feelings sound to us very much like contrivance:

Why then, O brawling love, O loving hate,
O anything, of nothing first create!
O heavy lightness, serious vanity,
Misshapen chaos of well-seeming forms,
Feather of lead, bright smoke, cold fire, sick health,
Still-waking sleep, that is not what it is!

(I.1.176–81)

We may well feel that Romeo is in love with the idea of being in love, and we have a good deal of sympathy with Benvolio's attempts to make him see sense and Mercutio's efforts to mock him from his moanings. We should remember that on stage the prospect of neither of Romeo's two friends taking his 'love' too seriously would strengthen our suspicions. Here is a very young man playing love games.

When Romeo sees Juliet, all this changes. All his extravagant avowals vanish in a moment. The speech in which Romeo first sees Juliet has a new simplicity and tenderness, a new wonder:

O, she doth teach the torches to burn bright!
It seems she hangs upon the cheek of night
As a rich jewel in an Ethiop's ear –
Beauty too rich for use, for earth too dear!
So shows a snowy dove trooping with crows
As yonder lady o'er her fellows shows.
The measure done, I'll watch her place of stand
And, touching hers, make blessed my rude hand.
Did my heart love till now? Forswear it, sight!
For I ne'er saw true beauty till this night.

(I.5.44–53)

That last line is a confession that all he said before was silly and wrong. Ironically, Benvolio had told Romeo that if he went to Capulet's party and saw Rosaline in the company of other ladies, he would realise she was not at all exceptional (I.2.93–8). Rosaline is indeed displaced, but by a sincerer and truer affection than Benvolio ever expected. The Friar is later amazed at Romeo's fickleness (II.3.61–76), but this is not the simple fickleness of a man exchanging one shallow love for another. It is a change from a shallow affection to a true affection. Although Romeo is always prone to lapse again into extravagant language, we never doubt the new depth of his feelings. He is, after all, constant to Juliet to death. Shakespeare stresses this change by making Rosaline only a name. We cannot take too seriously protestations of love for a woman we never see or hear.

Juliet also undergoes a change, but she is never presumptuous and silly like Romeo is in the earlier part of the play. She is modest, subdued, quite without knowledge of the nature and power of love when we first meet her. When her mother suggests that Paris might make a good husband, Juliet simply replies:

I'll look to like, if looking liking move.
But no more deep will I endart mine eye
Than your consent gives strength to make it fly.

(I.3.98–100)

For Juliet, the meeting with Romeo is an awakening to what love is, and with this she discovers a new resolution. She flatly contradicts her promise of obedience here by marrying Romeo secretly. And she emerges as a strong and practical personality – far more so than Romeo. In the balcony scene, she addresses Romeo directly and plainly, asking down-to-earth questions to which Romeo replies with elaborate images (for example II.2.62–9). When she discovers that Romeo has overheard her confessing her love for him, she does not deny it, but with startling and winning directness dismisses all the forms of courtship:

Thou knowest the mask of night is on my face,
Else would a maiden blush bepaint my cheek
For that which thou hast heard me speak tonight.
Fain would I dwell on form – fain, fain deny
What I have spoke. But farewell compliment!
Dost thou love me? I know thou wilt say 'Ay'.
And I will take thy word.

(II.2.85–91)

Shakespeare admired this kind of honesty: it appears in other of his heroines (for example, Miranda in *The Tempest*, III.1.48–91). And it is Juliet, we notice, who first mentions marriage, and sets Romeo on to arrange it (II.2.143–8). (Juliet's plain language is discussed on p.98.)

Thus, both hero and heroine undergo a clear change (although Romeo's is, perhaps, a return to his old self, see p.100). It is to make this plain that Shakespeare does not bring them together until the end of the first act. By then, we have got to know their characters and situation and can better appreciate the transformation that occurs. And seeing it, we cannot but admire their love, believe in its power, and sympathise with the lover's predicament.

Romeo and Juliet in relation to the other characters

Now, the easiest way to gain sympathy for a hero and heroine is to make them suffer at the hands of nasty and unpleasant characters. If everyone else in the play were evil, the hero and heroine would stand out more clearly. Our sympathies would be with them as 'right' and against everyone else as 'wrong'. Shakespeare, however, is more subtle than this. Romeo and Juliet are not entirely 'right', nor are the other characters entirely 'wrong'. Hence, we cannot simply say that we feel sympathy for Romeo and Juliet and detest all the people who put obstacles in the way of their love.

We have only to think of Paris, for example. Were he an old man or unsuitable in any other way, we should not hesitate to dismiss his suit to Juliet and to prefer Romeo's love to his. But he is not: he is young, agreeable and pleasant, an eminently suitable young man. His obsequies at Juliet's tomb in V.3 make it clear that he had a true affection for Juliet. And so we feel some sympathy for him as the rejected lover killed through no fault of his own.

Or we might think of Juliet's father, Capulet. Were he a villainous old man we could confidently hate him and extend all our sympathy to the wronged Juliet. He is certainly very cruel to Juliet in III.5, but that is not all there is to him. He is so angry then because he is bitterly disappointed. We know he has great affection for his daughter and hopes she will have a happy future (I.2.7–19). He believes she grieves for the death of her cousin Tybalt, and thinks that marriage to Paris will make her happy. This is why he agrees to the marriage without consulting Juliet (III.4.12–28), as Juliet's mother says and Paris later explains to the Friar (III.5.107–10; IV.1.6–15). He is angry when Juliet refuses in III.5 simply because his plans for her happiness are frustrated. Clearly, then, we cannot think of Capulet simply as a cruel father, a tyrant over his daughter. This means that we must be aware that Juliet does wrong in going against him, and that we feel some sympathy for him both when he thinks Juliet is dead (IV.5) and when she really is so (V.3).

Why does Shakespeare do this? Why does he prevent us from seeing those who bring about the death of the lovers as cruel and unpleasant people? The answer is partly that he knows too well what people are really like to simplify things like that. He knows no one is wholly good or wholly bad, and this awareness guides him as he characterises people in his plays. He is true to the facts of human nature. But he also does something more by preventing a simple sympathetic response. He is able, through these many characters each partly good, partly right, to explore many different ideas on love. *Romeo and Juliet* is a play about love, but in a fuller sense than that it is simply a play about two young lovers. The lovers are set in a world of real people who have ideas on the nature of love. And so we are able to see alternative attitudes to love to those of Romeo and Juliet. This poses questions in our minds. Instead of simply giving us two ideal lovers of whom we approve and other unfeeling characters whom we dislike, Shakespeare gives us a set of people whose remarks lead us to ask 'Are Romeo and Juliet right?' 'What is the value of love?' 'What is its nature?'. We can see in the play many different views of love struggling with one another.

Romantic and unromantic love

So we see in the play romantic and unromantic ideas of love in conflict. Romeo and Juliet are romantic. They give their all and disregard everything else. For Capulet, however, love and marriage are matters to be decided by a prudent father with the best interests of his daughter at heart. For Lady Capulet, Juliet's mother, it seems to be a matter of worldly wisdom. She is a rather curt, tart woman. She is not yet 30 years old (in I.3.72–4 she says she was a mother at about Juliet's age, and as Juliet is now nearly 14 this would make Lady Capulet about 28), yet her husband is an old man (I.1.90; I.2.3; I.5.22–5), well past the age for dancing (I.5.31–41). To him, Lady Capulet speaks abruptly, often reminding him of his age (for example I.1.76). She seems to have little love for him in the romantic sense (for example IV.4.11–12) and the difference in their ages leads us to suppose she married him not for love but for convenience. It was the sensible thing to do to get a good position in the world. Like Capulet himself, she has no patience with Juliet's refusal of her father's prudent scheme (III.5.203–4). Because of their views on love, neither parent can understand why Juliet should possibly want to decline such a handsome offer of marriage as Paris's.

In a different way, Benvolio is also sensible in his approach to love. In the early scenes of the play he tries to show Romeo that his affection for Rosaline is extravagant and unwarranted. He points out that if Romeo were to see her with other women he would realise she is nothing exceptional (I.2.85–6, 93–8). He does not treat Romeo's affection quite seriously, and wonders that Romeo can go through such agonies. We can appreciate this attitude: who has not remarked of a friend or acquaintance in love 'I don't know what he sees in her'? That Romeo's affection for Rosaline is not genuine does not affect the common sense of what Benvolio says. He would almost certainly have said the same thing about Romeo's love for Juliet had he known of it.

Spiritual and sexual love

Shakespeare, then, gives us prudent, sensible, worldly-wise attitudes to love, from people who have Romeo's best interests at heart. We cannot simply dismiss them. So, too, we see realistic and earthy attitudes to love in conflict with higher, more spiritual ideals. It is, when we first read the play, surprising to find so much bawdy talk, so many jokes about, and references to, sex. This is, indeed, how the play begins, with Sampson and Gregory making ribald jests – 'I will be civil with the maids,' says Sampson, 'I will cut off their heads' (I.1.21–2), meaning he will take their virginity. For these servants, the relationships between men and women are clearly a matter of sex only.

Throughout the play the love of Romeo and Juliet is set in a context of such lewd talk which pokes fun at love. The Nurse is forever making sexual puns and innuendoes. She repeats with relish her husband's joke when the baby Juliet falls down:

'A was a merry man – took up the child.
'Yea,' quoth he, 'dost thou fall upon thy face?
Thou wilt fall backward when thou hast more wit.
Wilt thou not, Jule?'

(I.3.41–4)

The point of the joke is, of course, that Juliet will lie on her back when a man makes love to her. Similarly, the Nurse anticipates the sexual pleasures of Juliet's wedding night with Romeo (II.5.75) and with Paris (IV.5.5–7) with the same glee. Indeed, that the Nurse can suggest that Juliet should go ahead and marry Paris even though she is already married to Romeo (III.5.213–26) shows that the Nurse has scant regard for loyalty or any of the usual virtues of love. Morality and high feeling mean little to the Nurse, who sees sex as the essential thing in the relationship between men and women.

Mercutio, too, has little patience with Romeo's high feelings. He has a down-to-earth remedy for Romeo: 'If love be rough with you, be rough with love' (I.4.27). He cannot see the sense of Romeo's 'dumps' and by his jokes constantly makes fun of Romeo's pretensions. He mocks Romeo's extravagant passion (II.1.6–21), and by his insinuations suggests it is all a fraud to disguise simple sexual passion (II.1.33–8). Once again, we know the Nurse loves Juliet dearly, and that Mercutio is Romeo's best friend. We cannot simply dismiss their views of love as those of unfeeling and unkind people.

Passion and moderation

Again, we see passion and moderation in conflict. The Friar, who as 'ghostly father' to both Romeo and Juliet is therefore much concerned for their spiritual welfare, often speaks against uncontrolled passion. It was, he says, that Romeo 'doted' on Rosaline, not that he 'loved' her, which he disapproved of (II.3.77–8). That is, he disapproved of unreasonable infatuation ('doting'), not what he calls 'love'. But, clearly, for the Friar love is a thing of moderation. Feelings should always be controlled. He does not like the sudden haste of the impetuous lover Romeo – 'Wisely and slow. They stumble that run fast' (II.3.90) – and is suspicious of great passion:

> These violent delights have violent ends
> And in their triumph die, like fire and powder,
> Which as they kiss consume.
>
> (II.6.9–11)

He directs Romeo to 'love moderately'. Such a love, he believes, will last (II.6.14–15).

Were Romeo and Juliet wrong?

These, then, are some of the conflicting attitudes to love in the play. The hero and heroine are surrounded not by villains but by well-intentioned and affectionate people who, all in their different ways, advise against extreme passion and unconsidered love. Their advice makes sense, the more so when we remember that Juliet herself was half-afraid that their love was too sudden to be sincere (II.2.116–20).

And in one way, of course, everyone else in the play *is* right. The romantic love of Romeo and Juliet does lead to their death. It is quite true that they act without forethought, without consideration of the consequences, that they are consumed by their love, and that the result is that they die. And to an Elizabethan audience it would have been plainer than it perhaps is to us that Romeo and Juliet did wrong to marry in secret without their parents' consent. This would have been a serious act of disobedience at that time. Indeed, Arthur Brooke had seen this as the point of the tragedy. In the preface to his poem, he explained that he believes Romeo and Juliet were justly punished for their immoderate passion and their defiance of proper authority in arranging a secret marriage. Brooke calls their love 'unhonest desire', and rebukes Romeo and Juliet for ignoring their parents and making use of 'dronken gosyppes' and 'superstitious friers' in order to satisfy their 'wished lust'. To his mind, they shamefully abused 'the honorable name of lawefull mariage' and thoroughly deserved to die for their 'unhonest lyfe'.

Is this what Shakespeare means us to think? Does he mean us to agree with the other characters in the play, and to condemn Romeo and Juliet? Are they justly punished?

The feud

The answer is, of course, no. The beauty of the scenes in which the lovers meet is in itself proof enough that Shakespeare wants us to respond wholly and totally to this love. Did he not want this, he would not have made it sound so attractive, nor would he have made Romeo and Juliet such appealing people. But there is a further significant element in the play which we have not yet considered and which affects our response. The parents that Romeo and Juliet defy are engaged in a feud. The love of the hero and heroine is set in a context of hate. This is an extremely important point to grasp. The play's first scene is concerned with this feud; we are made aware of it before ever we meet Romeo or Juliet. Indeed, it is the very first thing the Chorus mentions in the Prologue:

> Two households, both alike in dignity
> In fair Verona, where we lay our scene,
> From ancient grudge break to new mutiny,
> Where civil blood makes civil hands unclean.

> (lines 1–4)

And throughout the play we are constantly reminded of this feud. Although we do not know what began it (and so cannot take sides) it is of very long standing (an 'ancient grudge'). The 'fiery Tybalt', whom we meet in the first scene, is in the background throughout the early scenes of the play. We know he is determined not to let the matter of Romeo's intrusion into Capulet's party drop (I.5.91–2) and we fear the worst. And in III.1, the turning-point of the play, the worst comes about. The feud is directly responsible for the secret marriage, Romeo's banishment, and so for the Friar's scheme which leads to the deaths of the lovers. In short, it is hate which kills Romeo and Juliet in Shakespeare's play. It is only because they belong to enemy families that all the apprehension and secrecy are necessary. And only because of that do things go so badly wrong.

It may have puzzled us to understand why Shakespeare spends so much time on this feud, but now, perhaps, we can see what he was doing. Although everyone else in the play may be full of good sense, they are all also engaged in a feud which is the opposite of love. We cannot prefer their way of life to that of Romeo and Juliet, who want nothing to do with the feud. Romeo clearly does his very best not to become involved in III.1. Shakespeare here makes an effective alteration to the story as told in Brooke's poem. There, Romeo and Tybalt alone fight. By making Romeo refuse, only to be drawn in by the death of his friend Mercutio, Shakespeare makes it plain that Romeo was an unwilling combatant. In short, the world of Romeo and Juliet's love, in II.2 and III.5, seems a haven of peace and love, removed from all this brawling and hate.

The triumph of love

Shakespeare achieves more than this, though. We know that the Prince tries to stop the feuding, but in vain. We know the Friar hopes that the marriage of Romeo and Juliet may unite the families. He too, fails. Church (the Friar) and State (the Prince) cannot, with all their worldly wisdom, all their common sense, end the hatred. But, and here is the glory, the love of Romeo and Juliet *can*. Certainly they die, but their deaths make Capulet and Montague realise how wickedly foolish is their feud, and they are reconciled. We might be tempted to feel that the last part of the play, after the deaths of Romeo and Juliet, is an anti-climax. This is to misunderstand Shakespeare's intention. As the Friar explains at length the tricks and deceits Romeo and Juliet had been put to by their families' hostility for each other, shame grows in Capulet and Montague, and they realise what they have done. *They* have killed Romeo and Juliet. And this brings them together:

Capulet, Montague,
See what a scourge is laid upon your hate,
That heaven finds means to kill your joys with love.

(V.3.291–3)

The play ends here, with this reconciliation, and not with the deaths of Romeo and Juliet, because this means that *love triumphs*. To the feuding world of Verona, peace and harmony are restored by the fates of Romeo and Juliet. This is only possible (and this is the point) because Romeo and Juliet did *not* listen to anyone's advice. It was only because they were true to each other, that they defied the world and neglected its advice, that they were killed; and it was only because of this that hate finally died. Had the play ended with their deaths, all would have been lost; as it is, the play ends with positive gain. Had Shakespeare not dwelt on the feud, we would have had a play which showed love destroyed, a pessimistic play. As it is, though love is destroyed, it is not destroyed in vain. The whole drift of the play is thus to show that this love has a power, a beauty, an ability to heal old wounds, of which no one else's idea of love has any understanding.

Tragedy: foreboding and fate

This brings us to an essential characteristic of Shakespearean tragedy. It is the nature of tragedy to end in death and sadness, but a Shakespearean tragedy is never *only* sad. Shakespeare's tragedies are not pessimistic, hopeless plays. The audience does not feel that the deaths that end the plays have been pointless. Certainly, they are regretted; certainly, we wish things could be different; but we do not despair. This is the peculiarly agonised response a Shakespearean tragedy always evokes. We have just seen how *Romeo and Juliet* vindicates the lovers and that their deaths bring about reconciliation and peace. We are, at once, glad they did not die in vain, and sad they had to die at all. The two things go hand in hand: it is because Romeo and Juliet are the lovers they are that we wish they could live, and yet it is precisely because they are the lovers they are that they have to die. We can put it the other way: were they not such lovers they would have lived; but then, the feud would have continued too. This is the central irony of Shakespearean tragedy: we, in the audience, suffer because we so much want a happy ending even as we know that it is impossible, that, in a strange way, it is better that the protagonists die.

Fate in the play

In *Romeo and Juliet* it is quite clear that the lovers do have to die, that they are doomed. In this early play, Shakespeare has a simple conception of tragedy. The lovers are the victims of circumstances. They are not responsible for their fates: a terrible succession of mischances destroys them. Had any one of so many things been different, all would have been well. Had Friar Laurence's letter been delivered . . . had Juliet woken earlier . . . and so on. We noticed that these coincidences are hardly realistic (p.75), but they do serve an important dramatic purpose: because things keep going against the lovers we begin to feel that a hostile fate is working against them. Shakespeare deliberately encourages this view throughout the play.

Right at the start the Chorus tells us we are to see a 'pair of star-crossed lovers' (line 6) and from then on there are repeated ominous suggestions that Romeo and Juliet are fated to die. Even before

Romeo has seen Juliet, as he is about to join Capulet's party he says:

> . . . my mind misgives
> Some consequence, yet hanging in the stars,
> Shall bitterly begin his fearful date
> With this night's revels and expire the term
> Of a despised life, closed in my breast,
> By some vile forfeit of untimely death.
>
> (I.4.106–11)

He is, of course, right, and the audience, hearing these lines, fears as much. The moment after they have met, each lover has a similar foreboding that this love will end in disaster. When Benvolio says 'Away, be gone. The sport is at the best', Romeo replies, 'Ay, so I fear', meaning he fears things can only get worse from now on (I.5.119–20). And Juliet, learning Romeo's identity from the Nurse, says 'Prodigious birth of love it is to me/That I must love a loathed enemy' (I.5.140–1). In the balcony scene, when they declare their love, Juliet mistrusts this sudden passion (II.2.116–20). Romeo goes to marry Juliet with a challenge to Fate on his lips ('Then love-devouring death do what he dare' (II.6.7)), and an Elizabethan audience would know that Fate has a habit of accepting such challenges. As the lovers part, Juliet asks Romeo 'O, thinkest thou we shall ever meet again?'; Romeo tries to reassure her, but she replies:

> O God, I have an ill-divining soul!
> Methinks I see thee, now thou art so low,
> As one dead in the bottom of a tomb.
>
> (III.5.54–6)

The next time she sees Romeo he is, indeed, dead in the bottom of a tomb. Romeo's dream, which he recounts as he waits in Mantua for news from Verona, has a similarly ominous note: 'I dreamt my lady came and found me dead' (V.1.6). When Romeo hears the news of Juliet's death, he turns on Fate: 'I defy you, stars' he cries (V.1.24). As he looks on the dead Paris, he thinks of the two of them as the victims of circumstances, both written 'in sour misfortune's book' (V.3.82), and, as he prepares to kill himself, he says he will 'shake the yoke of inauspicious stars/From this world-wearied flesh' (V.3.111–12). And the Friar himself, who had tried to help these 'star-crossed' lovers, admits there was nothing he could do against the Fate which seems to have worked against them: 'A greater power than we can contradict/Hath thwarted our intents' (V.3.153–4).

References like these throughout the play (even if we do not notice them individually) gradually increase the air of foreboding and strengthen the impression, which the sad succession of hostile chances has given us, that there is nothing Romeo and Juliet can do. They seem helpless. The curse of a dying man was, to Elizabethans, particularly ominous, and the dying Mercutio cries three times 'A plague a'both your houses' (III.1.91, 99–100, 108). The point is plain.

One recurring kind of remark works particularly strongly to darken the atmosphere of the play. Time and again Shakespeare introduces the idea that Juliet will be the bride of Death. She herself first speaks like this the moment after she has first met Romeo:

> Go ask his name. – If he be married,
> My grave is like to be my wedding bed.
>
> (I.5.134–5)

When she hears of Romeo's banishment she looks at the ropes which were to have brought Romeo to her room, and resolves:

> He made you for a highway to my bed,
> But I, a maid, die maiden-widowed.
> Come, cords. Come, Nurse. I'll to my wedding bed,
> And death, not Romeo, take my maidenhead.
>
> (III.2.134–7)

Lady Capulet reminds the audience of this way of thinking about Juliet when she exclaims, in her anger at Juliet's refusal to marry Paris, 'I would the fool were married to her grave' (III.5.140), and Juliet's father, Capulet, speaks similarly when he thinks Juliet is dead:

> Death is my son-in-law. Death is my heir.
> My daughter he hath wedded. I will die
> And leave him all. Life, living, all is death's.
>
> (IV.5.38–40)

Paris, weeping at the vault, thinks that he grieves by Juliet's bridal bed (V.3.12), and finally, Romeo, preparing to join Juliet in death, and seeing her beauty, thinks Death loves her and this keeps her beautiful:

> Ah, dear Juliet,
> Why art thou yet so fair? Shall I believe
> That unsubstantial death is amorous,
> And that the lean abhorred monster keeps
> Thee here in dark to be his paramour?
>
> (V.3.101–5)

Remarks like these mean that death is always in the back of the minds of the audience; they encourage us to expect it to be the result of the lovers' affair and so impress on us the hopelessness of their situation.

Fate and character

In this play, then, Shakespeare's idea of tragedy is of a hostile Fate working against the lovers. Through no fault of their own, circumstances are repeatedly arranged to work against them. This is the old medieval idea of tragedy. In his later, great, tragedies Shakespeare was to move away from it. In plays like *King Lear* and *Othello* he explores the ways a man's own character contributes to his downfall. It is because Lear is the kind of man he is that he makes a wrong decision and so brings about his own death. It is because Othello is the kind of man he is that he believes Iago's false suggestion that his wife, Desdemona, is unfaithful, and so kills her. Certainly, in these later tragedies, the characters are not entirely to blame: there is always an element of chance. Circumstances combine with character: the hero is placed in just that situation which he cannot handle. In *Romeo and Juliet,* however, Shakespeare has not yet gone this far in exploring the relationship between character and Fate: as we have seen, chance is paramount. Although Romeo's impetuosity does contribute something to the tragedy (see p.101), it is not really the actions of the lovers which directly cause their deaths. Their marriage is not a wrong decision, as Othello was simply wrong to believe that Desdemona was unfaithful. It may have been an *unwise* decision to get married, but that is not the same thing. It is Fate which determines that the lovers should be born of enemy families, that Mercutio should be killed by Tybalt, that Friar Laurence's letter should not be delivered. This is what destroys them, and we pity them as innocent victims.

This is certainly how Romeo and Juliet speak of themselves. After killing Tybalt Romeo exclaims 'O, I am fortune's fool' (III.1.136), and later he speaks of his 'betossed soul' (V.3.76), suggesting that, like a helpless ship in a storm, he is blown hither and thither by Fate. And when she learns she must marry Paris Juliet exclaims in despair that she is the weak victim of Fate's schemes:

> Alack, alack, that heaven should practise stratagems
> Upon so soft a subject as myself!

> (III.5.210–11)

Shakespeare's presentation thus invites our sympathy, and is quite unlike the moral indignation we heard from Brooke a moment ago.

Style: wordplay and plain speaking

Linguistic changes

Shakespeare's friend and fellow playwright Ben Jonson claimed that Shakespeare 'was not of an age, but for all time'. When we first read a play by Shakespeare, particularly one like *Romeo and Juliet,* we may well wonder if this can be true. The first thing that we meet is the words on the page, and these can sometimes seem very odd indeed. Of course, they were written nearly 400 years ago, and, in time, words change their senses, colloquial expressions go out of fashion, idioms alter. Often a curious-looking line in Shakespeare can be explained in this way. The very first line of the play is an example: 'Gregory, on my word, we'll not carry coals'. Sampson and Gregory do not put a sack of coals down on the stage in disgust, nor does Sampson mean that he is not going to fetch any for Capulet! He is using a proverbial expression which has now fallen into disuse: his meaning is that he is not going to put up with any insults from the Montagues. The glossaries that follow each of the scene summaries in these notes will make clear how many such phrases there are in the play. Here is another example: Mercutio says to Romeo at one point, 'Tut, dun's the mouse, the constable's own word' (I.4.40). We need not be afraid to admit that, on first reading, this looks very like nonsense. Again, Mercutio is using a colloquialism that has gone out of fashion. His meaning is simply 'be quiet', 'stop talking like that'.

Lines like these look peculiar, and so we will try to discover their meaning. There is, however, a more serious danger, more serious because we may not be aware of it. Unless we remember that Shakespeare's language is certainly 'of an age' we are liable to forget that words he used which we still use may not have meant then what they mean now. Hence, a line may make good sense to us, and we may suppose we understand it, when in fact Shakespeare meant something quite different from the sense we take from it. Here is an example: when Tybalt is angry because Romeo has come to Capulet's party, Capulet tries to calm him, and says:

Here in my house do him no disparagement.
Therefore be patient; take no note of him.

(I.5.70–1)

Capulet does not mean that Tybalt should be patient, ignore Romeo now, and wait for another opportunity; he means quite the opposite, that Tybalt should be *calm* and forget about Romeo altogether. Here is another, slightly more complicated, example: Juliet, in the balcony scene, says to Romeo, 'In truth, fair Montague, I am too fond' (II.2.98). We understand 'fond' to mean 'affectionate', and so suppose Juliet is saying that she likes Romeo too much. 'Fond' did have this meaning in the Elizabethan period, but it also meant 'foolish' and that meaning is not excluded here. Juliet is saying that she may seem silly in liking Romeo so much so suddenly. Unless we realise the senses of the word 'fond' we will get only half the sense of the line. The student has always to be on the look-out for changes in sense of this sort.

Wordplay

As that last example shows, though, we notice something more than the changes in meaning time has brought about. Juliet's line was clearly written by a man who was alive to the ambiguities of words, the different senses they carry, and who wished to *use* these senses. When we write or talk we try to say as precisely as we can what we mean. Shakespeare, by contrast, seems often to want to carry on several meanings at once, and does not seem at all concerned to choose between them, to write clearly and exactly. A poet is someone who is aware of the suggestiveness of words, but, of all poets, Shakespeare is the one who is most aware of the ambiguities and nuances of words. Instead of shunning it, he delights in it and tries to use it. He does not tie words down: he releases them. He uses words with a kind of abandon, a joy in them merely as words, as things to play with. This can be very disconcerting for the reader unaccustomed to this taste, especially when it is an early play which is being read, for in these this trait is most apparent.

We notice it most plainly, of course, in that feature of the style of *Romeo and Juliet* which most disturbs a modern reader, the endless wordplay. We find characters quibbling with words, playing with their senses, making puns, from the very first lines of the play when the servants talk about 'coals', 'collier', 'choler' and 'collar' until the end. We do not now have much taste for the kind of·'wit combat' Romeo and Mercutio engage in in II.4, and it takes a good deal of study before we can make out what on earth they are talking about. Mercutio, of course, is the character most adept at playing with double meanings. Romeo cannot say the simplest thing without Mercutio twisting it. When Mercutio says, in the line we have just noticed, 'Tut, dun's the mouse', 'dun' is a pun on Romeo's simple statement 'The game was ne'er so fair, and I am done' (I.4.39–40). Romeo, though, can do it too. A little later in this scene, Mercutio observes that 'dreamers often lie', that is that they tell lies. Romeo wittily follows by taking 'lie' in the sense 'lie down' when he says 'In bed asleep, while they do dream things true'. Mercutio had made a complete statement; Romeo cleverly uses it as merely the introduction to his own point, which is the opposite of Mercutio's. And he does this simply by a play on the word 'lie' (I.4.51–2).

There are, of course, far more elaborate examples than this, but they are so common we need not bring any more forward here. Instead, let us consider the question, why did Shakespeare play with words like this? Part of the answer must surely be that he *enjoyed it.* Words were the tools of his trade, and he was skilful with them; in the pun, the quibble, double meanings and the like, he was showing off his skill. He would have been encouraged to do so by the taste of the time, for there was then far greater appreciation of this kind of skill than there is now. If we look, for example, at some of the love poetry of John Donne, written at the same time as *Romeo and Juliet,* we can see exactly the same kind of wordplay. It was regarded as 'witty writing'. 'Witty' did not mean then simply 'funny' or 'clever', as it does now, but also 'surprising'. And often, we can still see how the wordplay *is* comic, clever and surprising (for example the play on 'case' in IV.5.97–9).

We may accept comic use of the pun but Shakespeare was capable of indulging his verbal ingenuity at serious moments too. Sometimes it is very hard to see how the puns in such cases contribute to the effect. When Juliet is saying goodbye to Romeo she puns on the word 'division' (III.5.29–30). Her feelings are genuine in this passage, but to modern taste the wordplay introduces a note of false ingenuity.

In some serious moments, though, we can still see how the wordplay contributes to the effect. It may produce powerful compression of language: much is said in little space. For example, when the Prince says 'Throw your mistempered weapons to the ground' (I.1.87), he means that the weapons are badly tempered (or made) because they are used in bad temper by fellow citizens against each other. Or it may express confusion of feeling: when Juliet fears Romeo is dead, she puns on the pronoun 'I', the vowel 'i', the eye and the word 'ay' (III.2.45–50). Her lines effectively convey the fact that if Romeo is dead she too ceases to exist as a person, as a distinct 'I'. Later in this scene, Juliet strings together a list of oxymorons (III.2.75–6). The verbal conflict in these words of opposite meanings reflects Juliet's emotional conflict: she loves Romeo and yet is appalled at what he has done in killing Tybalt. Let us take one last example. In III.5, after Romeo has left, Lady Capulet comes to speak to Juliet. She believes Juliet grieves for the death of Tybalt, though we know Juliet is actually grieving for Romeo's departure. The two understandings are kept in play throughout the dialogue, Juliet meaning one thing and Lady Capulet taking a different meaning. Here, the verbal ingenuity underlines the gulf between mother and daughter. They are not talking *to* each other at all. Lady Capulet has no notion of what her daughter really means, any understanding of her true feelings, and this the audience realises since it does understand what Juliet means (III.5.68–102; the student might be helped by the notes to these lines).

The language of love

A different aspect of this delight in language is Shakespeare's use of the conventional diction of love poetry. We have noticed that Mercutio jests at Romeo as a follower of Petrarch (p.78), and in the early scenes Romeo is forever using the exaggerated and artificial language of late medieval and Renaissance love poetry. Shakespeare is here using language to show that Romeo's feelings for Rosaline do not run very deep. His speeches in I.1 and I.2 are too elaborate, too contrived to sound like true expressions of feeling. In a similar way, the over-obvious rhetorical patterning of the laments in IV.5. 49–64 prevents us from taking them too seriously.

But Shakespeare can use the conventions of love poetry to quite a different purpose. The sonnet was then the most popular form for love poetry. Sir Philip Sidney's sequence of sonnets *Astrophel and Stella* (1591) started a vogue, almost a craze. Every poet (including Shakespeare himself) turned out sonnets during the last part of the sixteenth century and the early seventeenth century. Shakespeare adopts this form and uses it in all seriousness in the play. When Romeo and Juliet first meet, their conversation is in the form of an Elizabethan (or Shakespearean) sonnet. This usually rhymed *abab cdcd efef gg,* although this example (I.5.93–106) repeats the second rhyme of the first quatrain to give *abab cbcb dede ff.* (There was another form also used at this time, called the Classical or Petrarchan sonnet, which rhymed *abba abba cdd cdd,* or *cde cde*). The essential point about the Shakespearean form is that it ends with a couplet, and so comes to a final climax. This form gives to the meeting the audience has been expecting a formality and dignity, as well as a lyrical quality, which elevates it. The rhymes give the lines a music, and as the form of the sonnet is completed in the final couplet, so the meeting comes to a climax, the courtship is completed, and the lovers kiss.

This is clearly a carefully designed 'set piece'. There are a number of other such set pieces in the play, carefully written speeches, which may even strike us as a little over-long. Examples are Mercutio's Queen Mab speech (I.4.53–95); Juliet's soliloquies as she waits for news of Romeo and as she prepares to take the potion (III.2.1–31; IV.3.14–59); the Friar's first soliloquy, his long speech to Romeo on moderation and patience, his explanation of his plan and his summary of the plot

(II.3.1–26; III.3.108–58; IV.1.89–120; V.3.229–69); and Romeo's soliloquy as he prepares for death (V.3.74–120). Here we are again confronted with the fact that this is not realistic drama: people do not speak at such length when they are alone, nor so carefully at emotional points in their lives. This is not realistic drama: it is poetic drama, and the Elizabethan audience seems to have delighted in, and appreciated, poetry in a way later audiences have not done. The way to respond to such pieces is not to ask whether people in this situation would really have talked like this; nor is it to ask whether the point made needs to be made at such length. These are not prose passages conveying only meaning, but, as poetry, passages which are working upon our sensitivities, our feelings, trying to create a certain mood, or response, in us to what is happening. They are the Elizabethan equivalent of the photographic and sound effects a modern film producer uses to persuade his audience to respond in a certain way to his film. We need, in other words, to try to surrender ourselves to the poetry.

Stylistic variety

We begin to see that there is a good deal of variety in Shakespeare's style in the play. We have noticed:

(*i*)   The use of colloquial idioms.
(*ii*) Punning for comic effect.
(*iii*) Wordplay for serious dramatic effect.
(*iv*) The use of the conventional language of love poetry, both mockingly and in earnest.
(*v*)   Formal and elaborate soliloquies and long speeches.

To these we may add:

(*vi*) The use of prose. Prose is the medium in all Shakespeare for comic characters and characters of a low position in society. So the servants, Gregory and Sampson, begin the play in prose. It obviously distinguishes them from the noble and more important characters who speak in more expressive and dignified verse. Prose is also used to show changes of feeling and mood. The comic banter at the beginning of II.4 is in prose, but later in the scene when, in more serious mood, Romeo plans his marriage,. he speaks in verse. In II.5 the Nurse moves in and out of prose according to the tone of her speech; when she finally gets to the important matter of Romeo's message, she settles on verse.
(*vii*) The use of rhyme. There is far more rhyme in this early play than in Shakespeare's later work. With the passage of time he came to

use blank verse (unrhymed lines of five stresses) almost exclusively. Rhymed verse obviously sounds more artificial than unrhymed (we notice the rhymes), and it limits the poet, who has to find a rhyming word at the end of each line. In *Romeo and Juliet* the rhyme is often incidental, but in II.3, for example, its use throughout the scene serves to remove the world of the Friar and his cell from the rest of the play, where people do not use rhyme so consistently. Rhyme may mark out key statements (for example III.1.119–20), and its formality of tone is used to distinguish important moments in the action, for example, when Romeo first sees Juliet (I.5.44–53) and the ending of the play. It may also register a decisive change in the action: so, when Romeo leaves Juliet, it is with a couplet (III.5.58–9). In all these cases (and many others, which the student may easily find) we notice the rhyming words and these alert us that something significant is happening at that moment.

(*viii*) Suiting of language to character. We may contrast the formality of Escalus's speeches with Mercutio's wit, and both of these with the Nurse's colloquial and wandering utterances. Similarly, variety in the language expresses the different moods of a character: in I.2 ·Capulet speaks calmly, but his disjointed speech towards the end of III.5 effectively conveys the heat of his emotions.

(*ix*) Imagery. *Romeo and Juliet* is remarkable for the evocative power of its imagery. This is another aspect of that delight in words mentioned earlier, and again marks out the play as an early work. There is an extraordinary richness in its figurative language. We notice this especially in the balcony scene, II.2, but it is there, in a different mood, in Juliet's soliloquy in IV.3 and as Romeo prepares for death in V.3. Shakespeare can conjure up exquisite beauty and horrible death, the beautiful and the grotesque, with equally vivid imagery. The metaphors can also be more subtle: Lady Capulet's elaborate comparison of Paris to a book sounds impossibly far-fetched and contrived, and so reflects the insincerity of her feelings. She is not really interested in Paris as a person at all. She wants to 'sell' Paris to Juliet as a highly desirable husband (I.3.80–95).

The student can pursue these hints as to the variety of Shakespeare's style by asking himself, as he reads, 'Why is this passage written like this? What is the effect of this particular image here? How do I respond to the quality of the verse here?' and so on.

Words and truth

There is one last interesting thing we may notice, which is a matter of theme as much as language. Throughout his career Shakespeare was intrigued by the relationship between words and truth. Often in his plays we find elaborate and involved language associated with hypocrisy and deceit, plain speaking with honesty and truthfulness. In *King Lear*, for example, the daughters Goneril and Regan, who do not love their father Lear, speak to him in ornate and contrived speeches; the third daughter, Cordelia, who does love him, speaks plainly and directly. The nobleman, Kent, who sides with Cordelia when Lear casts her off, also speaks bluntly and plainly; the courtier Oswald, who sides with Goneril in her quarrel with the king, speaks in the fashionable language of the court. When Lear himself comes to realise that it was Cordelia who truly loved him, and that Goneril and Regan had deceived him when they pretended to care for him, he too comes to speak plainly. (The interested student might look at *King Lear* I.1.34–187; II.2.1–122; IV.7.1–85.)

In the early play *Romeo and Juliet* we can see Shakespeare beginning to examine this idea. We have heard Mercutio mock Romeo for adopting the language of love poetry (II.4.38–43; see p.94), and Mercutio similarly mocks as false the assumed language of fashionable courtiers (II.4.28–35). The Friar makes a similar point. When Romeo comes to tell him of his new love for Juliet, the Friar loses patience with Romeo's elaborate metaphorical language, and begs Romeo:

> Be plain, good son, and homely in thy drift.
> Riddling confession finds but riddling shrift.

> (II.3.51–2)

At this Romeo at last gives over his conceits, and speaks directly:

> Then plainly know my heart's dear love is set
> On the fair daughter of rich Capulet.

> (II.3.53–4)

And the Friar suggests Rosaline had rejected Romeo precisely because his affected talk of love was seen by her as insincere, something memorised specially for the occasion:

> O, she knew well
> Thy love did read by rote, that could not spell.

> (II.3.83–4)

Above all, though, it is Juliet who is suspicious of words. In the balcony scene she rejects the affected language of courtship, that is, language which does not tell the truth about one's feelings ('farewell compliment' (II.2.89)); she beseeches Romeo to speak plainly ('O gentle Romeo/If thou dost love, pronounce it faithfully' (II.2.93–4)); and she stops Romeo swearing an elaborate lover's oath (II.2.109–11). Her frankness here reflects her sincere and unaffected feelings. Later in the play, there is a clear contrast between Romeo, still inclined to be fanciful, and Juliet. As they are about to be married, Romeo asks Juliet to describe their love, as he cannot do it:

> Ah, Juliet, if the measure of thy joy
> Be heaped like mine, and that thy skill be more
> To blazon it, then sweeten with thy breath
> This neighbour air, and let rich music's tongue
> Unfold the imagined happiness that both
> Receive in either by this dear encounter.

(II.6.24–9)

Romeo's language here – 'blazon', 'rich music's tongue' – shows the kind of thing he has in mind. Juliet, however, replies:

> Conceit, more rich in matter than in words,
> Brags of his substance, not of ornament.
> They are but beggars that can count their worth.
> But my true love is grown to such excess
> I cannot sum up sum of half my wealth.

(II.6.30–4)

Juliet is saying here that words, however elaborate, cannot possibly convey what she feels; and that she values the thing itself (her love) more than the ability to describe it. In other words, she sees Romeo's invitation as a pointless exercise. This distrust of fine-sounding words to convey anything truly will be a recurring theme in later plays.

The characters

The grouping of the characters

The action of *Romeo and Juliet* involves two carefully balanced groups of characters. At the head of the two feuding families of Verona are Lord and Lady Capulet and Lord and Lady Montague. Juliet, not yet 14 years old (I.2.9; I.3.11–15), is the only child and heir of the Capulets (I.2.14; I.5.112–7), as the youthful Romeo is of the Montagues (we hear of no other children, and V.3.210–11 suggests Romeo is an only son). As Juliet has a cousin, Tybalt (I.5.61;

III.2.66, 96), so Benvolio is Romeo's cousin (I.1.105, 159; II.1.3). These two cousins are clearly contrasted. When we first meet them, Tybalt starts a fight and Benvolio tries to keep the peace (I.1.63–71). This is characteristic. Throughout the play, the 'fiery Tybalt' (I.1.109) feels resentment and anger, while, on the other hand, Benvolio tries to prevent quarrelling and fighting (for example III.1.1–4, 49–52).

Furthermore, as the hero and heroine each have a cousin, so each has a close friend. Juliet's foster-mother and confidante, the Nurse, is balanced by Romeo's friend, Mercutio. Just as the old, easy-going and talkative Nurse is a contrast to the young and quiet Juliet, so the witty, intelligent and high-spirited Mercutio is a contrast to the passionate and often depressed Romeo.

The ruler of Verona, Prince Escalus, is set apart from both families, but his public commands to the two families to cease their feuding (I.1.81–103; III.1.186–97) are paralleled in their turn by Friar Laurence's secret attempts to unite Capulets and Montagues through the marriage of Romeo and Juliet (II.3.85–8). Outside each family, the Prince in public and the Friar in secret try to prevent that hostility which, in the end, kills Romeo and Juliet. The Prince as a ruler is concerned to stop 'mutiny' amongst his subjects, and the Friar, as a churchman, is also led by his office to try to stop it, but, although the Prince and the Friar are outside the families, each is connected to both, and so involved in their quarrelling personally: the Prince as the kinsman of Romeo's friend Mercutio and Juliet's suitor Paris (V.3.295; III.1.109, 145, 188–9) and the Friar as father confessor to both Romeo and Juliet (II.2.192; II.4.177–9).

And finally, all these noble figures are off-set by the servants of each household – it is, indeed, with the servants quarrelling in comic imitation of their masters that the play begins.

It is helpful if you realise that the characters are deliberately grouped in this way. They are not a casual collection of people, but figures brought together as part of a design. As Shakespeare creates characters he is not thinking of them primarily as *people,* but as parts of a dramatic pattern. He is concerned with how they will react together to gain dramatic effect. It is no accident that he develops Mercutio and the Nurse from his source (see p.19): he needs them as part of his design. This is why, in the history plays, Shakespeare does not feel bound to show accurately the personalities of his characters as they actually were in history. He gives them the personality which will serve his play. Indeed, though Shakespeare's characters are marvellously credible beings, realistic, we could say, we must be very careful in thinking about them as people. We have already noted that the plot of the play and the language of the play are not realistic (p.76). If we think of the characters simply as being realistic, then we shall wonder how the Friar could concoct such a plan as he does, or how Juliet can speak such long soliloquies. We must try to see the characters, too, as parts of the play.

If we approach them like this, then we can understand why Shakespeare grouped them as carefully as he did. It is by his arrangement of contrasts and comparisons that we come to know the characters better, and so appreciate what is going on in the play. We understand a thing better if we can contrast it with its opposite. So Juliet's youth and innocence are made clearer by the Nurse's age and rather immoral worldly wisdom; Benvolio's peaceable nature is made plainer by Tybalt's quarrelsomeness. And Shakespeare gains dramatic effect by constantly varying the pattern: Tybalt clashes with Benvolio in I.1, but with Mercutio and Romeo in III.1. By this same means, Shakespeare increases our insight into the characters. For example, we see Juliet not only with the Nurse, but with Romeo, with Lady Capulet, with her father, with the Friar. Each time she is presented in a new light and so we learn a little more about her.

And it is as parts of a design that the characters all have a typical quality. Each is a particular *kind* of person, readily recognisable, and as such he works in the play. Thus, the Prince is there primarily as a figure of authority and stability. He represents order – that order in society which the feud of Capulets and Montagues threatens. If we understand this, then we can see why it is fitting that it is the Prince who officially oversees the reconciliation of the families at the end of the play. His presence enforces the fact that order and harmony have been restored. A similar kind of general quality is present in all the characters: Romeo is the young lover; the Nurse the old gossip; the Friar the secret schemer whom Protestant Elizabethan England loved to imagine as typical of Roman Catholic Italy.

This is not to say that Shakespeare does not individualise his characters. He certainly does. The way they speak, their language, is very much their own, and they are given just those little features of personality which make them more than mere types. The following notes help to illustrate this, but you should remember that while Shakespeare brings his characters to life they are still parts of the play.

Romeo

When we first meet him, Romeo is a moody rejected lover, given to elaborate complaint about the pain caused by a love we suspect is not very deep (this was discussed on pp.78–9). But he had not always been like this, solitary and withdrawn. The very fact that his father, Benvolio and Mercutio all make so much of his changed 'humour' shows that his present behaviour is a drastic alteration and that he is not like the Romeo they used to know (I.1.118–57; I.4). We know that he is well thought of in Verona. Even Capulet, the head of the rival house, admits it (I.5.65–8). The most interesting thing Capulet says is that Romeo is 'well-governed': clearly, he was not always subject to such moods. The implication is that, before he became infatuated with Rosaline, Romeo was a popular, lively and sociable member of Veronese society.

It is therefore a testimony to the truth of his feelings for Juliet that, when he has arranged his marriage to her, he is like his old self. 'Now art thou sociable. Now art thou Romeo' exclaims Mercutio (II.4.87). Whereas the infatuation with Rosaline dulled him, Romeo's love for Juliet reveals his true liveliness. By this simple change, Shakespeare comments on the nature of the affections and, in Romeo's high spirits in II.4, shows us what a witty young man he really is.

Once he has ceased to brood, however, Romeo is clearly a rather impractical young man. He is all for impetuous action, but takes little consideration as to ways and means. Juliet has to point out to him that the marriage must be arranged; he is more inclined to express the rapture of his love than to plan what to do about it (II.2.139–48, 164–9). When he goes to the Friar, he is in a great hurry, but has no real suggestion to make beyond saying the Friar 'must' marry them (II.3.53–60). Later, when he meets the angry Tybalt, Romeo is at first moderate, but the death of Mercutio is too much for him: 'fire-eyed fury be my conduct now' he cries (III.1.124) and he throws consideration to the winds.

Impetuous and, impractical, Romeo is also more than a little passionate, as that last example suggests. When he hears of his banishment, he behaves very much like a child, throwing himself to the ground in a frenzy of grief (III.3.65–71, 84). He has here lost all self-control. It is the Friar who brings him to himself and shows him what he now must do (III.3.109–59). It is entirely characteristic that when, in Mantua, he hears the news of Juliet's death, he reacts immediately, without waiting a moment to consider what is the best thing to do. As he rushed into marriage, collapsed into grief, so now he decides instantly to return to Verona to kill himself (V.1.24–6).

The passion and impetuosity that lurk in Romeo are his most distinctive features, and, to an extent, they are responsible for the tragedy which overwhelms the lovers. Had he been a little less hasty, less impassioned, all would have been well. A little delay in V.1 would have given time for him to learn the truth about Juliet's 'death'. On the other hand, it is this same quality which allows him to give himself so entirely and completely to Juliet. It is characteristic of Shakespeare that the same trait is at once the thing we admire and the thing we regret, both the source of what is good and what is bad in a character.

Juliet

Juliet is a much quieter character than Romeo. We have noticed how she begins the play as a submissive and obedient girl who has lived a sheltered life (see p.80) and that she develops into a resolute woman. Romeo's character does not so much change: rather, we find out what he is really like. But Juliet *does* change, she does develop. In this respect, she anticipates the characters of Shakespeare's later plays. And the mature Juliet is a contrast to the impassioned Romeo. Her love is as deep as his, and as deeply felt (notice how she longs for the return of the Nurse at the beginning of II.5, and anticipates her wedding night in III.2). We are quite wrong if we suppose there is anything insipid or weak about her feelings, but she has more aware-ness of the practicalities of the situation than Romeo and she speaks much more frankly (see p.80).

She contrasts with Romeo in another way, too. There was an element of self-deceit in Romeo's role as Rosaline's lover. Juliet, as her plain speaking shows, is above all honest, with both Romeo and herself. Because of Romeo's banishment she is reduced to playing a part, the part designed for her in the Friar's plan. But she never becomes less than true to herself. Deception is not her nature, and nothing less than her love for Romeo would have prompted her to deceive her parents. That she does so is a measure not of how deceitful she is but of how independent and firm-minded she has become. She recognises only one obligation – to Romeo.

This aspect of her character is enforced by the fact that she is gradually isolated from everyone she knows and loves. This, indeed, happens to Romeo too, but he is away in Mantua throughout Act IV and it is Juliet we actually see struggling alone with circumstances. She is without Romeo; cut off from her parents because they do not know of her marriage; even the Nurse lets her down by suggesting bigamy when Juliet turns to her for help. We should notice that Juliet is thus abandoned by everyone in the one scene, III.5, which begins with Romeo leaving. These repeated desertions are cumulatively very striking. Juliet's exclamation 'Ancient damnation!' (III.5.236) marks the final break with all the guardians of her childhood. She is now alone, a tragic heroine: 'My dismal scene I needs must act alone' (IV.3.19).

Friar Laurence

The Friar is the one person to whom Romeo and Juliet can turn throughout the play. Everyone speaks well of him, and we have noticed that his is the voice of moderation in a stormy and violent world (p.84). He is a pleasant and likeable figure, but not a very fully developed one. He is chiefly important as the means to promote the plot. We can see this if we begin to ask serious questions of him. Should he have agreed to a secret marriage? Should he have deceived Juliet's parents? Don't his words to them in their grief when they think Juliet is dead sound like hypocrisy – he is certainly not telling the truth (IV.5.65–83)? Doesn't he treat Juliet's parents cruelly, putting them to this suffering? These questions we might ask a *real* friar: we cannot ask them of Friar Laurence. The Prince's verdict that he is a holy man (V.3.270) has to be accepted as a convention of the play, however much we might wonder what kind of holiness it is that can do what Friar Laurence does. In a case like this, talk of the realism of Shakespeare's characters can only mislead.

Juliet herself comes up against this difficulty. At one point in the play, as she is about to take the potion, she raises moral questions about the Friar, that is, she treats him as a real human being with motives for his actions. She wonders whether, as he has already married her secretly to Romeo, he has actually given her poison to take so that she will die and no one will know of what he has done. This we might well suspect of a *real* friar who had acted like Friar Laurence. But Juliet puts aside the worry with the rather unconvincing reflection that he *must* be a holy man:

> What if it be a poison which the Friar
> Subtly hath ministered to have me dead,
> Lest in this marriage he should be dishonoured
> Because he married me before to Romeo?
> I fear it is. And yet methinks it should not,
> For he hath still been tried a holy man.
>
> (IV.3.24–9)

Juliet here uses almost the same words as the Prince in the last scene of the play, reasserting the type that the Friar represents. We can almost see Shakespeare's interest in human beings developing at this moment in this early play. He has used the Friar as a plot device; Juliet has grown into a living being, and so she thinks about the Friar as a human being would. This results in a clash between a real being, who asks questions, and a type-figure who behaves as he does for no very convincing reason.

Mercutio

Mercutio is important in the play as a foil to Romeo and as providing comedy, but, much more fully developed than the Friar, he is also a winning personality in himself. Gay, lively, always talking, jesting even in death (III.1.96–9), he is a clear contrast to Romeo, but his is an independent mind such that he wins our attention in his own right. We have seen he offers us an attitude to love worth considering (pp.83–4) and, although always witty, his is not an empty wit. Mercutio always has a point to make. We agree with the thrust of a good many of his jokes against Romeo early in the play, and his caustic comments on Italian duels and fashionable courtiers mark him out as one who, though 'the life and soul of the party', can view experience objectively (II.4.19–35). Even so, his intelligence and shrewdness do not prevent him from being killed. We remarked earlier that Shakespeare brings Mercutio into the duel in III.1 in order to show Romeo's unwillingness to fight (p.86), but this incident also shows Mercutio has deep feelings, and, what is more, feelings which can be misguided. In so assiduously pursuing the feud, in feeling Romeo has 'let the side down' by refusing to fight Tybalt, Mercutio shows a false sense of honour which, ironically, will contribute to the death of his friend. Mercutio had seemed to turn the play into a comedy at times: it is with his death that we know this is to be a tragedy.

The Nurse

The Nurse is Juliet's equivalent of Romeo's Mercutio. Like Mercutio, she does not change or develop; like him, she supplies a good deal of humour; like him, she has an attitude to love which contrasts with that of the hero and heroine (see p.83); and, like Mercutio, she is almost entirely Shakespeare's invention, being barely mentioned in the sources. We may not be quite sure how to take her: vulgar, coarse, quite insensitive and immoral, she can be made to sound like an old witch.

Certainly, her wordiness can be very infuriating. She speaks a good deal and says very little (notice how long it takes her to say how old Juliet is in I.3 and to tell Romeo what she has come for in II.4). This can sometimes seem like a deliberate wilfulness: in II.5 she seems to have little regard for Juliet's feelings as she delays giving Romeo's message. Her garrulousness is a clear contrast to Juliet's unequivocal directness. When Juliet has something to say, she says it directly (with these examples from the Nurse we might compare Juliet's speech to the Friar in IV.1.50–67).

The Nurse contrasts with Juliet in another way, too. Once she has met Romeo, Juliet knows exactly what she thinks and what she wants. The Nurse, on the other hand, changes her mind with bewildering rapidity. She seems to support Lady Capulet in her praise of Paris (I.3.79), and then helps Juliet arrange her marriage to Romeo (II.4). After Tybalt's death, she agrees when Juliet, in her astonishment, raves against Romeo as deceitful (III.2.85–90); but when Juliet recovers herself, the Nurse readily undertakes to bring Romeo to her (III.2.138–41). She warns Romeo and Juliet of the approach of Lady Capulet in III.5, and yet, at the end of that scene, she much prefers Paris to Romeo ('Romeo's a dishclout to him') and suggests Juliet should marry Paris (III.5.213–26). And although she helped to bring about the marriage to Romeo, she is quite happy to wake Juliet in IV.5 for her marriage to Paris. In short, the Nurse agrees with whatever seems to be the opinion of the moment.

And yet the Nurse is not an old witch. Certainly, sex, child rearing and old memories make up a good deal of her conversation. She is quite without refinement, but she is also without affectation. She speaks plainly of the basic things of life she knows. If we dismiss her as a meddlesome old woman we show ourselves less sympathetic than Shakespeare, who has given her an obviously genuine love for Juliet (for example in I.3.60–3) and a position of trust in the Capulet household. We may be sad that she lets Juliet down at the crucial moment (III.5.205–43), but we can hardly blame her for that. She is advising what seems to her, truly, to be the best course of action, and, although she does not know it, she is more than punished by losing Juliet's confidence. This is something that would hurt her deeply. Indeed, that the Nurse does not understand the depth of Juliet's love for Romeo, and so can suggest marriage to Paris, is a measure of how far Juliet has grown up. She is no longer a little girl whom the Nurse can influence; now she is a woman with a commitment beyond the Nurse's comprehension.

Capulet and Lady Capulet

These characters are considered in the discussion of the themes of the play, pp.81–2.

Benvolio and Tybalt

These simple characters, the peacemaker and the quarreller, are obvious contrasts. They behave according to type throughout the play, and have none of the liveliness or individuality of Mercutio or the Nurse. Tybalt is *always* angry (I.1.65–71; I.5.54–92; III.1.34–132; these are the only times he appears in the play). He seems to think it is up to him to keep the quarrel alive. He takes Romeo's appearance at the party as a personal insult and determines to avenge it. By contrast, Capulet and Montague, the older men, seem inclined to let the quarrel drop (for example in I.2.1–3; I.5.54–88).

Benvolio concerns us a little more, as the friend who persuades

Romeo to say why he is so depressed. But thereafter he is always for peace, and rather overshadowed by Mercutio and Tybalt. He is clearly a foil to them, and so vanishes from the play after III.1. With both Mercutio and Tybalt dead, Benvolio is no longer needed as part of the design. That Shakespeare is so willing simply to drop a character from the play, without explanation, shows that he is thinking in terms of design, in terms of the usefulness of the characters.

Paris

Paris is not the unpleasant opposite to Romeo we might expect (see p.81), but he is very different from Romeo. Whereas Romeo is passionate and impetuous, Paris is calm and decorous. He acts as a suitor to a young lady ought to act. Against Romeo's impetuosity, he offers us the normal form of courtship. He does not steal into the lady's garden at night, nor does he visit her room secretly. He approaches her father with a proper proposal (I.2), and, when the father offers him his daughter's hand, he accepts it, even though he knows the daughter has not been asked (III.4). Indeed, it seems that Paris has never even spoken to Juliet: all his wooing has been to Capulet. (By contrast, Romeo has spoken *only* to Juliet, not to her father.) Thus, Paris serves to exemplify a very different kind of love from Romeo's. His proper course of courtship seems a rather pallid thing. His affection lacks passionate involvement, and, in paying scant heed to Juliet's own wishes ('That "may be" must be, love, on Thursday next' (IV.1.20)), seems to lack respect for the loved one.

But we should not be too hard on Paris. Shakespeare, clearly, could not develop Paris's love too much, or the audience would have been distracted from Romeo and would have begun to see Juliet as torn between two equally eligible young men. As it is, we see a different kind of love offered, and one which, though it may seem pale beside Romeo's, is not necessarily insincere. When Paris does meet Juliet in IV.1 he treats her with some consideration and tenderness, and his obsequies in V.2 suggest a genuine affection. And, like Romeo, he wishes to lie with Juliet in death (V.3.72–3). Furthermore, his courage in V.3, when he fights Romeo, should prevent us from dismissing him as a weak and unfeeling person.

Part 4

Hints for study

THESE NOTES have tried to explain something of the artistic character of *Romeo and Juliet*. We have seen that, as a product of the English Renaissance, written for the Elizabethan stage, the play has a very distinctive character. It is quite unlike the writing with which we are familiar today. Only by recognising this can we begin to discuss the play in a worthwhile way. So we should do all we can to understand Shakespeare's method, so that we do not deliver criticisms which are ill-informed and unjust because they miss the point. Examples of such criticisms might be: 'No one would trust the upbringing of his daughter to a character like the Nurse'; 'The Friar's scheme is quite incredible'; 'Mercutio's wordplay is boring and irrelevant'. It is by reflecting before we make comments of this sort, by trying to see the *purpose* of the play's apparent peculiarities, that we deepen our appreciation of it.

Our appreciation should try to be as inclusive as possible. The best understanding of a literary text is the one which can most satisfactorily explain all the features of the work. So we need to try to get as clear a view as we can of what *kind* of play we think this is, and then endeavour to see how each aspect of it fits in with this view. For example, if we think this is a tragedy, why is there so much comedy in it? If this is a play about love, why is there so much quarrelling? It is the firmness of the overall grasp of the play which determines the merit of any discussion of it, or essay on it.

As these examples show, it is by asking questions that our understanding of a literary work grows. It is a good plan to pause frequently as we read, to ask ourselves questions like 'why does Shakespeare introduce this character here?' 'why does he follow the last scene with this one?' 'what would be the effect of this passage in the theatre?' 'why do I feel like this when reading these lines?'. If we fail to ask such questions, we will find that we have drawn little from our reading. The play may have affected us, but we will be unable to say how or why.

Questions

The following are examples of the kind of questions on the play a student may expect to meet. They have all been touched on in these notes, and considering them may help the reader to get clear in his own mind how he thinks the play works.

Structure and plot

(1) Analyse Shakespeare's presentation of any turning-point in the play, and discuss its importance to the play as a whole.
(2) What does the time-scheme contribute to the play?
(3) Is the reconciliation of the families at the end of the play an irrelevant anti-climax?
(4) Examine some examples of Shakespeare's use of dramatic irony, and show what they contribute to the play.
(5) Illustrate some of the ways in which the nature of the Elizabethan stage has affected the structure of the play.

Themes

(6) What is the importance of the feud in the play?
(7) Examine the different views of love presented in the play, and discuss the dramatic reasons for their inclusion.
(8) Does Shakespeare intend us to approve of the love of Romeo and Juliet?
(9) Discuss the Friar's warnings against uncontrolled passion.
(10) Why does Shakespeare begin the play by introducing the love of Romeo for Rosaline?

Tragedy

(11) The Chorus refers to Romeo and Juliet as 'star-crossed lovers'. Do you agree with this view?
(12) Discuss the function of foreboding in the play.
(13) How far are Romeo and Juliet themselves responsible for their fate?
(14) As the hero and heroine both die, would you agree that this is a pessimistic play?
(15) Does the amount of coincidence in the play contribute to, or detract from, the power of the tragedy?

Poetry

(16) Discuss, and give examples of, the variety of Shakespeare's verse in the play.
(17) Discuss the merits and demerits of Shakespeare's use of wordplay.
(18) Illustrate the ways in which language is suited to character.
(19) Analyse Shakespeare's use of the conventions of Elizabethan love poetry in the play.
(20) Discuss the dramatic effectiveness of the soliloquies in the play.

Characters

(21) Would you agree that the characters are all essentially types?

(22) Analyse the development in the character of Juliet. What are her most important traits as a tragic heroine?

(23) Discuss the ways in which character contrasts contribute to the effect of the play.

(24) Why does Shakespeare introduce the characters of Mercutio and the Nurse?

(25) Do you think the Friar is a holy man or a deceitful schemer?

These questions have been divided up like the Commentary in Part 3 of these notes, but we should always remember that categories like 'structure' and 'theme' only exist for the convenience of critical discussion. They are not separate things in the text itself. That is a single whole, and so we find that any one of our convenient categories will always lead to another. For example, Juliet's contribution to the theme of the play depends upon what kind of person she is, and that is bound up with the way she speaks. Here, theme, characterisation and language all combine. We must try to remember that a work of art is an organic whole like this. Indeed, we can say that the more completely satisfying the work, the more difficult it will be to isolate any one particular feature of it from the others. It is only in bad writing that the rhymes, let us say, are painfully obvious. But we do have to distinguish different aspects of a text if we wish to talk about it. The categories used in the Commentary should help the reader to pinpoint the main features of *Romeo and Juliet*.

In preparing answers to questions like those given above, we need both to marshal our points in an orderly way and to support them with references to, and quotations from, the text. The reasons for this are simple: only if we present our points in an orderly fashion will our argument make sense, and only if we bring forward our evidence can we prove that our argument is sound. Without order, no sense of the play as a work of art can be conveyed: without quotations, our views lack conviction – there is no proof. A safe plan to follow in essays is (*i*) explain our understanding of the question; (*ii*) explain how we intend to deal with it; (*iii*) follow through this programme in order; (*iv*) conclude what we have established. This will ensure that the reader of the essay knows what we are trying to do. The method is illustrated in the two specimen answers that follow on pages 111–17.

References

As far as quotations are concerned, most of the important lines in *Romeo and Juliet* have been mentioned in the course of these notes. For convenience, some of them are listed below: the reader may like to look them up as a revision exercise to see whether he can explain their significance; help should be found in the relevant section of the Commentary.

KEY SCENES: I.1; I.5; II.2; III.1; III.5; V.3

CONTRASTING SCENES: II.6 and III.1; IV.3, 4, 5

DRAMATICALLY IRONIC SCENES: III.4; III.5.64–125; IV.4; the beginnings of III.2 and V.1

RHYME: Prologue; I.1.171–2, 185–99, 208–24, 237–8; I.2.16–37, 45–50, 85–6, 91–100; I.3.84–5, 97–100, 105–6; I.4.44–52; I.5.44–53, 58–63, 89–109, 134–44; II.1.Chorus; II.2.123–4, 154–7, 184–93; II.3; II.4.77–8; III.1.119–20, 174–97; III.2.130–7; III.5.23–36, 58–9; IV.5.96–144; V.1.85–6; V.3.12–17, 301–10

PROSE: I.1.1–62; I.2.38–44; I.3.101–4; I.5.1–16; II.4; II.5.38–45, 55–7; III.1.4–48, 76–80, 95–103; IV.2.1–8; IV.5.94–5

SOLILOQUIES: II.3.1–26; II.5.1–17; III.2.1–31; IV.3.14–59; V.3.74–120

LINES OF FOREBODING: Prologue, lines 5–8; I.4.106–11; I.5.119–20, 134–5, 140–1; II.2.116–20; II.6.7, 9–11; III.1.91, 99–100, 108, 136; III.2.134–7; III.5.54–6, 60–4, 140, 210–11; IV.5.38–40; V.1.6, 24; V.3.76, 82, 153–4

THE LOVE OF ROMEO AND JULIET: Romeo's speeches in I.1 and I.2; Juliet's submissiveness, I.3.98–100; Romeo's first view of Juliet, I.5.44–53; the wooing, I.5.93–110; the balcony scene, II.2; Juliet waiting for news of Romeo, II.5; the marriage, II.6; Juliet awaiting her wedding night, III.2.1–31; Juliet's response to the news of Tybalt's death, III.2.36–143; Romeo's response to his banishment, III.2.1–108; the parting of the lovers, III.5.1–64

VIEWS OF LOVE: the servants: I.1.1–30. Benvolio: I.1.225–38; I.2.81–100. Mercutio: I.4.27–32; II.1. Capulet: I.2.4–19; III.4; III.5.126–96. Lady Capulet: I.3.64–100; III.5.104–25, 203–4. the Nurse: I.3.40–9, 60–3, 68–9, 76–7, 79, 96; II.4.158–200; II.5.68–77; III.5.213–26; IV.5.1–8. Friar Laurence: II.3.27–90; II.6.9–15

Before we come to the specimen answers, one last point should be made. Of course a student will want to be well informed, but once he has done all he can to master the nature of the text, he should trust to his own responses. Literary discussion is not a science. Certainly, we can carefully scrutinise and describe features of the text, but our final verdict is not a scientific fact but a matter of personal appreciation. Literary discussion is mere mimicry if we only repeat what others have said about a text. We should always try to read the opinions of others *critically,* and decide for ourselves whether we agree with them or not (and that certainly includes the reading of these notes). We should try to be honest with ourselves, and give our own feelings about a text. It is, as we all know, not easy to be honest; it is much easier simply to do what we have been told, to follow others. But it is by trying to understand our *own* feelings as we read that we ourselves grow as our knowledge of literature grows. And, furthermore, it is personal commitment and insight which enlivens essays and marks them out as the work of an individual and sensitive mind.

Specimen answers

Discuss the dramatic effectiveness of the soliloquies in *Romeo and Juliet*

Romeo and Juliet has been called one of Shakespeare's most poetic plays, and in this early work there is clear evidence that Shakespeare delights in his skill with words. Punning and quibbling are common, and Shakespeare explores the resources of language to express extreme feelings of both joy and love, and despair and sorrow. There are a number of long speeches in the play which show this mastery of language. They serve to further the plot and reveal the character of the speaker (for example, the Nurse recollecting Juliet's childhood in I.3, the Prince commanding peace in I.1 and the Friar telling Romeo to control himself in III.3). Soliloquies proper (that is, speeches spoken by a single character alone on the stage) are slightly different in their dramatic purpose. They may forward the plot, but they are chiefly important for what they reveal of the mood and feelings of the speaker at that moment in the play. If we remember the close intimacy between audience and actors in the Elizabethan theatre, we can see why the soliloquy should have become an established dramatic convention. It does not work nearly so well in a theatre where the proscenium arch rigidly separates audience and actors. In Shakespeare's theatre, a character could reveal himself to an audience, take it into his confidence, as it were, because the spectators were all around him. It is as though we overhear the character thinking. We can see this if we look at three examples from the play. The three chosen come from different parts of the play, and each is spoken by a different character. This will help to show the variety of Shakespeare's use of the soliloquy.

It is in II.3 that we first meet the Friar. He is to play a significant part later, and so Shakespeare uses the soliloquy which opens the scene to show the audience what kind of man the Friar is. After this speech, we know him much better and what to expect from him. We are thus prepared to accept his later actions. The first thing we notice is that the speech rhymes. There is a good deal of rhyme in the play, but such a long rhymed speech stands out. The rhymes are noticeable, and give a certain formality to the lines. As we notice that the Friar speaks in a different form from that of the characters in earlier scenes, so we realise that we have moved to a different world of experience. (Shakespeare uses prose in the same way.) The rhymes thus serve to underline the fact that the Friar is a religious man, apart from the boisterous world of the rest of the play.

This is plain in what he is about to do as he speaks. He is going out early in the morning to pick plants from which to make medicines. This is a quiet, humble task, and the Friar speaks of it lovingly and knowingly. He sees the properties of the plants as evidence of the divine order of things. All things, he reflects, can be used for good. But also, all things can be perverted to evil ends. The Friar, then, although living in a 'close cell', is aware of evil in the world. But he talks of it calmly, without the passion of a Tybalt. This prepares us for the fact that he is ready with a solution when Romeo and Juliet each visit him for help. As he is not involved, he can think when they are caught up in emotion. The Friar's concern with plants also prepares us for the fact that he could make such a potion as he later gives Juliet.

At the end of his speech, the Friar reflects that men are like plants: they too have good and evil in them, as plants may contain harmful and medicinal properties. His speech ends as he remarks that if the 'worser' predominates then evil overtakes the man. This idea relates to one of the concerns of the play. The feud threatens to consume people like Tybalt, and does actually kill him and Mercutio (and also Paris, who challenges Romeo as a Montague). Yet Tybalt is not a bad man; he has been 'strained' from his good nature.

The Friar never speaks briefly. It is part of his character to be a little long-winded, and we can see this here. He speaks unhurriedly, and without elaborate imagery or rhetoric. This is appropriate: the Friar is a plain man, and his style of speech conveys this.

Very different is Juliet's soliloquy at the beginning of III.2. Here she is waiting impatiently for her wedding night. The speech does not forward the plot at all, but it tells us a good deal about Juliet. In particular, it emphasises the strength of her feelings. As Romeo is the more obviously passionate of the lovers, we might be inclined to suppose Juliet's love is weaker than his. This speech (like the one in which Juliet waits for the Nurse's return) corrects this view. The young Juliet anticipates her wedding night not with the glee of the Nurse, nor with the bawdy humour of Mercutio, but with deep emotion. Hers is a full-blooded love, and yet not one bound up only with the body and sex. Shakespeare is careful to show us that sex is part of full love; Romeo and Juliet do consummate their marriage in the course of the play, but sex is not all their feelings involve.

The language of the speech conveys both this passionate excitement, and a slight apprehension. Juliet both welcomes the coming night, and is a little afraid of it. 'Gallop', the first word of the speech, is a firm, commanding opening, suggesting haste. 'Fiery-footed steeds' continue the idea of speed, and add a suggestion of hot passion in 'fiery'. The references to Phoebus and Phaeton add something exotic to the mood. The tone changes, however, as Juliet goes on to think of the 'amorous rites' of the night. She is still young enough to blush at the thought. Yet she bids night 'come'. The way the word 'come' is repeated through the speech, like a refrain, conveys her longing. And what the night means to her is suggested in paradoxes like 'thou day in night', contrasts like 'snow upon a raven's back' and images like Romeo being cut into little stars. The language here, unlike the Friar's, is ornate, but deliberately so. It conveys a sense of richness, deep feeling (the stresses on night, secrecy and blood all tend in this direction), something awful and beautiful.

Thus, this speech shows us what the coming night means to Juliet. Shakespeare here, by his poetry, shapes his audience's response to the love of Juliet. After hearing this, although the plot has not moved, our knowledge of Juliet's love is much greater. There is, though, an ironic undercurrent through the whole speech. We know that Romeo is banished, and that the joy Juliet anticipates will be short-lived.

When Romeo prepares for death we get a very different kind of soliloquy, though again its main purpose is not to further the plot. As he opens the vault, Romeo is struck by Juliet's beauty. It seems to him that death has no power over her, that she is not dead. Ironically, this is of course the truth. We know that he is about to cut himself off from her for ever. He believes he is about to join her. Thus Shakespeare stretches the audience on a kind of rack. We want almost to cry out to Romeo that she is not dead, that he should not kill himself. The length of the speech itself increases this anguish in the audience, by giving them longer and longer to appreciate the full horror of what is happening.

The imagery here is again rich (Juliet has 'sucked the honey' of Romeo's breath) but also disturbing. The 'lean abhorred monster', as death is called, conjures up an image of a skeleton in our minds, and the idea of this figure being Juliet's 'paramour' is horribly grotesque. 'Worms' are now Juliet's 'chambermaids'. The unexpected linking of two things not usually mentioned together has just such a startling effect as Shakespeare's imagination often creates. The idea is again grotesque. The vault has become Juliet's bed-chamber, worms her maids, and there Romeo will lie with her. (This is the culmination of the idea of Juliet as being married in death that has run through the play). That Romeo can contemplate such a thing is explained when he goes on to talk of his 'world-wearied flesh'. All through the play Romeo has been a victim of adverse circumstances; he has been 'Fortune's fool'. Now, he has had enough: death seems to offer release from the torment of 'inauspicious stars', relief and peace, and above all, reunion with Juliet. So he longs for 'A dateless bargain to engrossing death'. That line, with its long vowels, sounds slow and long, like the idea it conveys. Romeo, now a 'desperate pilot' no longer able to sail between the obstacles Fate places in his way, will shipwreck his 'seasick weary bark'. 'Sick' and 'weary' repeat and en-force the idea of 'world-wearied flesh', and emphasise how much sad experience Romeo has gone through in the brief time-span of the play.

So we can see in these three examples that the nature of the poetry changes to convey the different moods and feelings of each moment. Each speech serves to deepen our appreciation of what that moment in the action means. It is, hence, by such speeches that Shakespeare's plays become more than mere stories. Through such techniques as that of the soliloquy, they become works of art with significance. And we also see how tragic irony can play through the lines, so that the audience's response is not a simple one of understanding, but one of being involved in the play. We have our own feelings because of our privileged knowledge of the situation.

Analyse Shakespeare's treatment of any turning-point in the play, and discuss its importance to the play as a whole.

Romeo and Juliet is a play with a single plot and a simple structure. Unlike *Henry IV, Part I,* or *A Midsummer Night's Dream,* for example, where Shakespeare follows the interlocking fortunes of several groups of characters, or *King Lear,* where two separate stories go forward together, here the play focuses clearly on the swift course of the love of Romeo and Juliet. This simple design begins hopefully, with all going well for the lovers, up to their secret marriage in II.6. However, there have already been several hints of tragedy to follow, and in the next scene, III.1, the tragic counter-movement begins. In this scene Romeo kills Tybalt. As a result of this, Romeo has to flee to Mantua. No sooner has he left than Juliet is faced with the new problem of the proposed marriage to Paris. The Friar endeavours to solve this with his scheme of the potion, but Romeo is wrongly informed that Juliet is really dead, and all is lost. We thus have a clear pivot in the action at III.1 (stressed by the fact that Mercutio, the merriest character in the first part of the play, then dies). But a number of other scenes also stand out as turning-points (although, interestingly, the actual marriage in II.6 is not one of them). The first meeting of Romeo and Juliet, and their wooing in the balcony scene are obvious examples. However, here we will look at III.5, as it is a long scene interesting in its own right, and one which is crucial to the action. We will first briefly analyse it, and then summarise its significance.

The scene begins with Romeo and Juliet parting. They met only on Sunday, and this is but dawn on Tuesday; yet this parting is no slight thing. Shakespeare's presentation of their love is such that we know the wrench it is for the lovers. This is enforced here, in the tender and beautiful language given to the lovers. Juliet knows it is dawn, and yet does not want to believe it. Romeo admits the truth in lines of delicate and evocative beauty:

> It was the lark, the herald of the morn:
> No nightingale. Look, love, what envious streaks
> Do lace the severing clouds in yonder East.
> Night's candles are burnt out, and jocund day
> Stands tiptoe on the misty mountain tops.
> I must be gone and live, or stay and die.

(III.5.6–11)

We should notice that this is quite unlike the exaggerated rhetoric Romeo can use. These images are natural, unforced, and the structure of the lines is simple and straightforward: they are thus far more haunting than Romeo's earlier extravagant exclamations about Rosaline.

This mood is abruptly broken as the Nurse interrupts the lovers to say that Lady Capulet is coming. We knew from the previous scene that she was to come, and we know why. That Capulet has arranged Juliet's marriage to Paris gives this opening part of the scene an added poignancy. We know, and Juliet does not, what is in store. This also makes Romeo's reference to 'jocund day' ironic. What follows is to be far from 'jocund'.

The lovers finally part. As they leave, there is one of Shakespeare's characteristic suggestions of tragedy to come:

> O God, I have an ill-divining soul!
> Methinks I see thee, now thou art so low,
> As one dead in the bottom of a tomb.

(III.5.54–6)

This is indeed how Juliet will next see Romeo. And she goes on to speak of him as the subject of Fortune, another characteristic reference in this play. Such remarks present the lovers as the helpless (and innocent) victims of circumstances. We more than suspect, because of such lines, that Juliet will never see Romeo alive again. This, of course, yet further increases the pathos of the parting.

The mood changes abruptly as Juliet and Lady Capulet engage in a kind of sparring match. Lady Capulet believes Juliet grieves for the death of her cousin Tybalt, but we know she grieves for the departed Romeo. Throughout the following dialogue there is a double meaning. Lady Capulet supposes Juliet refers to Tybalt when we know she means Romeo. This is dramatically ironic. The audience, in a privileged position of knowledge, understands more than Lady Capulet. It also stresses the fact that Lady Capulet does not know her daughter.

Lady Capulet then tells Juliet of the marriage to Paris which has been arranged. Juliet is, of course, dismayed. When Capulet enters to find out how she takes the news, there is another, startling change of mood. When he finds she refuses the proposal, Capulet erupts into anger. Hitherto we have seen him only as a solicitous and rather jovial father. Now we see him in an entirely new light. It is a good example of a character surprising us completely. Some may think that the characterisation is inconsistent, and that the Capulet of I.2 and I.5 could never behave like this. On the other hand, we have never seen Capulet crossed before, and so do not really know how he might behave in that situation. Furthermore, he is disappointed in his hopes for Juliet's happiness. Even so, we should perhaps add that in this scene Shakespeare is working to engage our sympathies for Juliet, and so it suits his purpose to have her father treat her cruelly here.

After this eruption, Juliet is left with the Nurse. Juliet is in great distress, and turns to the Nurse for help. The Nurse, we know, has been Juliet's life-long companion and confidante. It was she who helped to arrange the secret marriage to Romeo. Yet now, when Juliet most needs her help, the Nurse lets her down. With no understanding at all of the depth of Juliet's love for Romeo, the Nurse calmly suggests that, as Romeo is unlikely to be able to return, Juliet should go ahead and marry Paris. We have just seen Romeo leave Juliet, her mother fail completely to understand her, her father threaten to cast her off. Now, in the same scene, her last hope, the Nurse, fails her. This is a very powerful cumulative effect. A succession of disappointments leaves Juliet finally quite alone.

This scene, then, has remarkable variety of mood and effect. It is typical of Shakespeare that it is constantly surprising us, and that it works together to one end. This purpose will be clear if we look now at the significance of the scene. First of all, it is the last time the lovers are alive together on stage. Though we do not know this as we watch, we suspect it, because of Juliet's lines quoted above. Thus, in a sense, we take our leave of the lovers as they take their leave of each other. Secondly, the scene introduces the second major difficulty placed in the way of the lovers. Tybalt's death was the first (if we except the feud itself). That sent Romeo away. No sooner has he gone than Juliet is left alone to face the marriage with Paris which bursts upon her that very moment. (It is characteristic of this play that events come one on top of each other.) That 'alone' suggests the third part of the scene's significance. In the course of the scene Juliet is gradually deserted by Romeo, her mother, her father, and finally the Nurse. Happening in the one scene, this is powerfully dramatic. It is the last stage in Juliet's development into a tragic heroine, alone with her fate.

Thus, we could say that this scene seals the tragedy. It isolates Juliet, and with its ominous lines, dramatic irony, and a new twist to the plot, it hurries the play along the path begun in III.1 with Tybalt's and Mercutio's deaths.

Part 5

Suggestions for further reading

The text

There are four currently available editions of *Romeo and Juliet* which may be consulted with profit: they are listed below in their order of usefulness for the student not far advanced in Shakespeare studies.

SPENCER, T.J.B. (ED.): *Romeo and Juliet,* New Penguin Shakespeare, Penguin, Harmondsworth, 1967. This has an excellent introduction, and very full and helpful notes in the commentary which follows the text. There is also a discussion of the textual problems of the play.

BRYANT, JR., J.A. (ED.): *Romeo and Juliet,* The Signet Classic Shakespeare, New English Library, London, 1964. A useful introduction and glossaries on the same page as the text, which saves the reader having to refer to the back of the book. There is no commentary on the text, but there are helpful excerpts from critical studies of the play and a discussion of the text and sources.

WILSON, J.D., AND DUTHIE, G.I. (EDS.): *Romeo and Juliet,* New Cambridge Shakespeare, Cambridge University Press, Cambridge, 1955. The introduction to this scholarly edition of the play is readable and very helpful, and there is a valuable glossary, but the notes are designed for the mature reader of Shakespeare. For those interested in textual questions, there is an excellent discussion of the text, and also a stage history of the play.

FURNESS, H.H. (ED.): *Romeo and Juliet,* New Variorum Edition of Shakespeare, Dover Publications, New York, 1963. First published in 1871, this edition collects in notes on the same page as the text all the relevant comments of earlier editors. The 1597 quarto of *Romeo and Juliet* (Q1) is printed as an appendix. It is an edition to consult on particular points, rather than one to use as a main text.

General works on Shakespeare

HALLIDAY, F.E.: *A Shakespeare Companion 1564–1964,* Penguin Books, Harmondsworth, 1964. An encyclopedia of Shakespeare: alphabetically arranged entries cover nearly everything to do with Shakespeare's life, times and plays. A very useful work to consult on factual questions.

MUIR, K., AND SCHOENBAUM, S. (EDS.): *A New Companion to Shakespeare Studies,* Cambridge University Press, Cambridge, 1971. A collection of essays by different scholars covering such things as Shakespeare's life, the Elizabethan theatre, Shakespeare's English, his social and historical background. Very useful as an introduction to Shakespeare studies.

ONIONS, C.T.: *A Shakespeare Glossary,* second edition, revised with enlarged addenda, Clarendon Press, Oxford, 1958. A dictionary of Shakespeare's English, which explains the meanings of all words either not now in use or used in a different sense.

SCHOENBAUM, S.: *William Shakespeare: a Compact Documentary Life,* Clarendon Press, Oxford, 1977. The most authoritative biography.

Sources of *Romeo and Juliet*

BULLOUGH, G. (ED.): *Narrative and Dramatic Sources of Shakespeare,* 7 Volumes, Routledge, London, 1957–73, Volume I. Reprints Arthur Brooke's poem *The Tragicall Historye of Romeus and Juliet.*

MOORE, O.H.: *The Legend of Romeo and Juliet,* Ohio State University Press, Columbus, Ohio, 1950. A full account of the development of the Romeo and Juliet story.

SPENCER, T.J.B. (ED.): *Elizabethan Love Stories,* Penguin Books, Harmondsworth, 1968. Reprints William Painter's version of the Romeo and Juliet story.

Critical studies of *Romeo and Juliet*

Essays on the play may be found in the following books:

BROOKE, N.: *Shakespeare's Early Tragedies,* Methuen, London, 1968. Discusses the patterning of the play in language and structure.

BROWN, J.R., AND HARRIS, B. (EDS.): *Early Shakespeare,* Stratford-upon-Avon Studies III, Edward Arnold, London, 1961. Includes an essay by John Lawlor on the nature of the tragedy in *Romeo and Juliet.*

CHARLTON, H.B.: *Shakespearean Tragedy,* Cambridge University Press, Cambridge, 1949. *Romeo and Juliet* as an early Shakespearean tragedy which begins to show the characteristics of the later great tragedies.

DICKEY, F.M.: *Not Wisely But Too Well: Shakespeare's Tragedies of Love,* Huntingdon Library, San Marino, 1957. Ideas of love in the play.

GRANVILLE BARKER, H.: *Prefaces to Shakespeare,* 2 Volumes, Batsford, London, 1958, Volume 1. Especially on how the play might best be presented in the theatre.

HARRISON, G.B.: *Shakespeare's Tragedies,* Routledge, London, 1951. To show that Romeo and Juliet was, in 1595, the finest tragedy yet written for the English stage, Harrison follows the course of the play with analytical comments; a very useful introductory essay.

LERNER, L.(ED.): *Shakespeare's Tragedies: An Anthology of Modern Criticism,* Penguin Books, Harmondsworth, 1963. Includes extracts from M.M. Mahood, *Shakespeare's Wordplay* (London, 1957), an excellent discussion of the quibbling and punning in the play, and C. Williams, *The English Poetic Mind* (London, 1932).

MASON, H.A.: *Shakespeare's Tragedies of Love,* Chatto & Windus, London, 1970. Discusses particularly the relationship between Shakespeare's treatment of love and the tragedy.

STOLL, E.E.: *Shakespeare's Young Lovers,* Oxford University Press, London, 1937. A fine essay on the characters of Romeo and Juliet, the nature of their love, and how Shakespeare meant us to respond.

VYVYAN, J.: *Shakespeare and the Rose of Love,* Chatto & Windus, London, 1968. Ideas of love in the play.

The author of these notes

N.H. KEEBLE was educated at St David's College, Lampeter, and the University of Oxford. He was a Lecturer in English Literature at the University of Aarhus, Denmark, before taking up his present position as Lecturer in English at the University of Stirling in Scotland. He has edited Richard Baxter's *Autobiography* for Dent's Everyman University Library Series (1974), and published *Richard Baxter: Puritan Man of Letters* (Clarendon Press, Oxford, 1982) as well as a number of articles on late medieval and Renaissance literature. His edition John Bunyan's *The Pilgrim's Progress* for Oxford's World's Classics Series WCS published in 1984. He is also the author of the York Notes on Shakespeare's *Richard II*.